WITH

Acclaim for ~~Brain Storms~~ ...

An emotionally enriching book. It's a real page turner. A compelling "must read" for lay people as well as mental health professionals. Dr. Field presents an engrossing example of how a spontaneous past life regression made sense of a patient's present day fears and phobias.

—Constance Dean Yambert
President, Constance Dean Yambert & Associates

Brain Storms! is a fascinating account of soul transmigration that lends support to the notion that a soul's previous experience can affect and even wreak havoc in the next life. This book emphasizes the importance of not only acknowledging our ancestry but also the influence the spirit world may have on our current journey on this planet.

—David Cumes, M.D.
Author of *The Spirit of Healing*

An amazing journey, as patient and therapist break the time and space barriers for health and healing.

—Athena Sawyer, Ph.D., Clinical Psychologist
Author of *Peanut Butter and Jelly*

Only so often does a book come along that sparks the imagination and challenges the skeptics into a new way of thinking if not re-evaluation of what is possible. Now appears the insightful and provocative *Brain Storms!* by Dr. Field and Shawn Regan whose mystical journey leads us further into recognition that there is a good chance that some people have lived more than once. And, or, the hero of this book is recognition of this past created for him, an irrefutable past, and perhaps a never ending future.

—John Brady, Ph.D., Forensic Psychologist
Author of *Drug Addict*

It's warm , it's wonderful, it's uplifting, and so very inspiring. This book is chock full of discovery and insights. The growth and healing are miraculous. And it's written with wit and compassion.

—Patricia Fripp, CSP, CPAE
Past President, National Speakers Association

This book is a must read! The compelling story of a somewhat tenuous, and even frightening venture into a past life is beautifully written by the subject, Shawn Regan, with expert step by step commentary from his therapist, Dr. Eleanor Field. The unveiling, and gradual awareness, of minute details of a life lived in the early 1900's enabled Shawn Regan to heal frightening symptoms that almost paralyzed him from the benefits of his present day opportunities. Finally, the patient was not only cured of psychological symptoms but of possible life threatening physical ones as well. The expert guidance through the mental mine field by Dr. Field is documented simultaneously by patient and therapist. This book provides an important guideline for both therapists and subjects alike.

—Jeanne Avery
Author of *Past Lives, Present Loves*

Brain Storms!

Out of a Torrential Past
Into a Triumphant Future

a True Story

SHAWN REGAN AND
ELEANOR S. FIELD, PH.D.

TRANCE-FORMATION PRODUCTIONS
TARZANA, CALIFORNIA

Published by: Trance-Formation Productions

BRAIN STORMS!
Out of a Torrential Past
Into a Triumphant Future
Shawn Regan and Eleanor S. Field, Ph.D.

5567 Reseda Blvd., Suite 115
Tarzana, CA 91356 USA
(800) 56-hypno
info@DoctorElly.com
www.DoctorElly.com

ISBN 0-9717973-0-7
Printed in the United States of America

Publisher's Cataloging-in-Publication
(Provided by Quality Books, Inc.)

Field, Eleanor S.
    Brain storms! : out of a torrential past, into a
triumphant future / Eleanor S. Field and Shawn Regan ;
book design, Pamela Terry ; illustrations, Julie Welch.
--1st ed.
    p. cm.
    LCCN 2002101967
    ISBN 0-9717973-0-7

    Regan, Shawn—Pre-existence. 2. Reincarnation—
Biography. 3. Reincarnation therapy. 4. Intimacy
(Psychology) 5. Regan, Shawn--Health.   I. Regan.
Shawn. II. Title.

BL520.R44F54 2002   133.9'01'35092
                        QB133-748

Book Design by Pamela Terry, Opus 1 Design
Illustrations by Julie Welch

10 9 8 7 6 5 4 3 2 1
First Printing

Dedication

To my parents, Goldie and Louis P. Siegal,
whose guidance, love, and support ignited the light
which continues to brighten my mind.
May this book illuminate their heavenly spirit,
and may God's light continue to shine upon them.

To my husband, Boris, with love,
for his dedicated assistance
in the development of this book.

To Julie Welch,
for her imaginative cover and chapter illustrations.

To Pamela Terry,
for her graphic design.

To my daughter, Noreen,
who assisted in the editing.

To my patient, "Shawn Regan,"
whose devastatingly painful experiences
were transcended by his courage in continuing therapy
and realizing transformation.

Eleanor S. Field, Ph.D.

To John Williams, with whom it all began.

To Doctor Elly, whose trance-formations
brought me out of the Pit of Despair.

To Deborah, and the Crowning Celebration
of this journey ...with all my love.

Shawn Regan

"The soul is mightier than space,
stronger than time,
deeper than the sea,
and higher than the stars."
—Barbara Young,
This Man from Lebanon: A Study of Kahlil Gilbran

"A little while,
a moment of rest upon the wind,
and another woman shall bear me."
—Kahlil Gibran, *The Prophet*

"I hold that when a person dies
His soul returns to earth;
Arrayed in some new flesh disguise,
Another mother gives him birth.
With sturdier limbs and brighter brain
The old soul takes the road again."
—John Masefield

"...it retranslates them (religious themes, myths, stories)
from the language of imagined facts into a mythological idiom;
so that they may be experienced, not as time — conditioned,
but as timeless — telling not of miracles long past, but of
miracles potential within ourselves, here, now, and forever."
—Joseph Campbell

Introduction

Is birth the beginning and death the end? Can there be some form of consciousness after death? Is there such an entity as the soul, and can it transcend person, place, and time?

For a patient suddenly and surprisingly to experience episodes from an earlier life...

And for the initial event to occur spontaneously and dominate the patient so powerfully that today's self is completely suppressed for a given time while in a state of trance or hypnosis...

And for the occurrences which were encountered to be so powerful and meaningful that...

They illuminate the trials and tribulations in his present life...

And for these brilliantly relived encounters and the vividly expressed emotions and descriptions...

To result in a complete transformation of his present day personality...

And for this to resolve his phobias, fears, and even his physical problems...

What an astounding, rewarding passage...a mystical, magical journey to behold...

This is a true story. Every event actually occurred as presented here. To ensure privacy and confidentiality, the names of the patient and his significant others were changed. With tongue in cheek, my patient and co-writer chose the pen name of Shawn Regan, who was a character in the classic movie, *The Big Sleep*, starring Lauren Bacall and Humphrey Bogart. Poignantly, this character never actually appeared in the film.

This book is compiled out of video tapes, patient records, and Shawn's personal journal, which he kept during our working together. Each chapter begins with Shawn's sharing his escapades from his perspective; I then present the therapist's point of view on these episodes.

With an intense acting out of his feelings, Shawn Regan, the hero of this book, colorfully **lived** each past life adventure as John Williams. This phenomenon is called "revivification" or reliving. As Shawn's therapist and guide, I witnessed these escapades as they emerged. I felt as though I were there with him, caught within the web of what was occurring. As the adventures unfolded, the role enactments, along with the expressed rage, anger, sadness, and fear were heart rending. Each journey took me along with it. I too was hypnotized by what was happening. I never made suggestions which could influence that which was occurring. I did not wish to color or even shade the emerging episodes. Only when the feelings became tremendously overwhelming for Shawn, did I suggest that he move on and complete the scene or return to the safety of the present. However, in the chapter, *On the Train*, as an intuitive therapeutic endeavor, I participated in the trance as a passenger. This was for the purpose of promoting communication between us for better understanding of his thoughts and feelings.

More and more, our culture is turning to spirituality, and with that, credence has been given to past and future lives. Celebrities like Shirley MacLaine have popularized these concepts. A prolific writer, her book, *Out on a Limb*, has been a best seller for many years. The idea of lessons learned in one life's influencing another is held by many. Recent authors, like Gary Zukav, include the rebirth of the soul and reincarnation as an integral part of their philosophies. Zukav declares that "Personality...creates energy imbalances that are not able to right themselves within its own lifetime." Jeanne Avery writes about "the evolutionary process of the soul." In *A Soul's Journey*, a text about the return of Holocaust victims, Ms. Avery emphasizes empowering one's present life through past life regressions.

Various cultures have long believed in survival after death or reincarnation. Their beliefs have embraced many diverse and intriguing theologies. Hinduism emphasizes "Karma" or that your behavior in one life influences your next life. Some Hindus believe that people reincarnate as animals. The Druse of Lebanon, Israel, Syria, and Jordan hold that rebirth occurs immediately after death and behavior in one life has no effect upon the next. One is rewarded or punished only on "Judgement Day." The Igbo of Nigeria look for birthmarks which indicate wounds from a previous life. When a baby dies, that baby is believed to be reincarnated into the same family. In countries where Buddhism is practiced, belief in reincarnation permeates one's everyday life. Buddhists reincarnate until one no longer has desires and passions. He then reaches a state of "nirvana". In Hassidic Judaism, there are mystical stories emphasizing reincarnation. In Tibet, a search is conducted among young children for a new Dalai Lama, the embodiment of the same soul.

The sheer excitement of Shawn's journey and the fantastic behavioral changes which resulted were a reward to me, his therapist. I now want to give a gift to you, the reader. The dynamics of this case may further your thinking processes about past lives, and their influence on present behavior. The innovative techniques and hypnotic procedures with which I treated Shawn have already been received with interest by other therapists.

Shawn's insightful journey dramatically changed his life and also transformed my thinking about life, death and the hereafter. Join in our hero's adventures, and become immersed in his *passage into the past*. Allow it to inspire you and shine a measure of *light and lessons* upon your life, as well!

"Dr. Elly"
Eleanor S. Field, Ph.D., Clinical Psychologist

Table of Contents

Brain Storms!

A True Emotional Journey
Out of a Torrential Past
Into a Triumphant Future.

Prologue

Fact, fiction, or fantasy—
Does it really matter?
When one discovers the source
In another life even sadder.

Rain, clouds and wind
Wove into serpent-like terror.
And finally physical pain
Takes our hero on another road, even barer.

Neither of us had held
That when a person dies,
He would again live
Bearing a different disguise.

The tragedies of the soul
From the time before
Requesting resolution
By peering into a later door.

One day, while doing hypnosis
To manage his physical pain,
This hero spontaneously
Flashes onto another plane.

That road was dark and treacherous;
It gave him so much pain
But neither patient nor therapist
Could presuppose the gain.

**Through the passage of time
And into the past
His soul found the answers
To this life...at last.**

I

Brain Storms!

I

BRAIN STORMS!

*A bayonet wound in a past life
cuts to the heart of a present day nightmare*

Suddenly it was 1917. The only light was from the constant flashes of cannon and gun fire. The ear-splitting sounds of war were all around me - explosions, rifle shots, the whine of artillery shells soaring overhead. I was standing in a long trench, ankle deep in mud, shivering almost uncontrollably, as much from the piercing cold rain as from the fear of sudden death. To either side of me were my fellow British infantrymen, firing a steady spray at the barely visible enemy. I kept my head down as low as I could as I tried unsuccessfully to free my jammed rifle. I turned to my right, hoping to get one of the lads to help me, when the silhouette figure of a German soldier suddenly loomed up before me. I saw the outline of his spiked helmet and the gleam of his fixed bayonet an instant before he leaped into the trench and stabbed me in the chest. I cried out in agony. I was sure I'd been killed.

I continued to writhe and scream as Dr. Field worked to bring me out of the hypnotic trance she'd induced. She had quite a time of it – this had never happened in any of our previous sessions. Indeed, I learned later that it had never happened at all in the many years she had been in practice. Finally she got me back to the here and now. I was conscious, but still shaken at the terrifying, vivid experience I'd had. I still had a sharp pain in the upper right part of my chest where I'd been "stabbed". And I was totally baffled. "What the hell was that all about?" I wondered, as Dr. Field continued to soothe me with relaxation suggestions.

Finally, after several minutes, I was able to tell her in detail what I'd experienced. It had all been triggered by a hypnotic technique the doctor had never used on me before. As she gave me a verbal induction, she'd made several passes over my head and shoulders with her hand, only slightly touching my upper right chest, just below my collar bone. That was when all hell broke loose.

I was now wide awake, but my chest still hurt. Together we tried to figure out what this profoundly shattering experience had to do with the problem for which I'd consulted her. And also, we both speculated on whether indeed this had been a genuine past life experience.

Up to that time, there had been no suggestion whatever during my many visits with Dr. Field of taking me back to another life. We had explored, under hypnosis, my childhood experiences that might relate to the reason why I'd sought her help in the first place – a phobia I had developed about the weather – especially wind and rain.

This crippling fear seemed to come out of nowhere during the rainy California winter of 1992-93. Like every normal person, I've never been a fan of bad climate. But I'd never been terrified by it either. For some utterly confounding reason, I'd somehow gotten to the point where I'd scream out loud, stomp my feet and punch my fists into walls at the approach of a light shower. The pitter-patter of rain on the roof, which I was sure would leak in and drown me, and the sound of wind, which I felt might blow me away, scared the living crap out of me. I'd become completely fixated, unable to think about or do anything else except try to block out the sights and sounds of Mother Nature until the sun came out. Then I'd start worrying about the next storm. The only thing that would relieve my debilitating fear was a heavy dose of tranquilizers. But, of course, that did nothing to get at the cause of this puzzling ailment. And as soon as the numbness wore off, there I'd be again – a complete mess.

Clearly I couldn't go on like this. So I pulled out the Yellow Pages and looked under "Hypnotherapists". I chose to consult a doctor who specialized in hypnosis because I'd had some luck several years earlier with Arthur Ellen, a lay hypnotist who worked a lot with sports figures. At that time I'd developed a chronic backache from swinging a baseball bat. No doctor or chiropractor had been able to help me. But Arthur Ellen did – and in an astonishing way. He put me in a light trance and had me stand up and sit down several times. Then he declared that my back pain was gone. And it was! And not just for that moment, but for good. Remembering that experience gave me hope that hypnosis might be the right approach for me this time as well. I was in no mood for a protracted regimen of analysis. I needed relief fast or I feared I'd do something really crazy.

So I sought out Dr. Eleanor Field. I knew nothing about her except that her office was reasonably close by. On entering her waiting room, I was immediately impressed by all the certificates on the wall. Dr. Field was not just another shrink – she was a bona fide expert in hypnotherapy. She was a clinical psychologist, and a marriage, family therapist. She was a published author and taught other doctors how to use the techniques of hypnosis in surgery and pain management. Just what I needed, because I had a lot of pain to be managed.

Tuesday, November 10, 1992

As I sat waiting for Dr. Field to finish with the patient ahead of me, I tried to figure out how and why I'd gotten my head stuck in this bizarre emotional meat grinder. Why was I, Shawn Regan, a mature, middle-aged man, suddenly terror stricken by every turn in the weather? I felt like some tortured character in a Stephen King novel, not a professional animated cartoon writer. How could someone who'd spent his entire adult life trying to make people laugh suddenly find himself so totally miserable? I tried to think of any traumatic experience I might have had in my past that was associated with rain, wind, etc.. No typhoons, no hurricanes, no monsoons. I'd grown up in Chicago, the "windy city", where the climate can be as awful as any place on earth. But I couldn't recall ever having been afraid of the weather when I was a kid. Years later, during some heavy rains, one room of my home in Sherman Oaks, in the San Fernando Valley of Los Angeles, became flooded. That was very unpleasant and highly upsetting, but that had happened more than a decade earlier, and I no longer lived in that house. Then I thought, maybe it wasn't rain itself – maybe it was some other bad experience with water. I flashed on the time I fell into a lake at age six and nearly drowned. Because of that I'd had an extreme fear of getting in over my head until I was eighteen when a lifeguard friend finally taught me how to swim. But since then, I swim regularly and consider myself better than average in the pool, so that couldn't be it, either. No – whatever the reason for this recent state of weather/rain/wind panic, it was hidden deeply beneath my awareness.

I was actually glad that there was no window in Dr. Field's waiting room. As I entered the building on that grey afternoon in November, 1992, the sky had started to cloud up. It was comforting to know that if it began to rain again I wouldn't be able to see it – at least not until after my appointment I started to breathe a sigh of relief at that thought, but it stuck in my throat as the door to Dr. Field's office suddenly opened. I don't know what I expected her to look like – perhaps a tweedy, matronly, bookish version of your basic stereotypical psychiatrist or maybe a new-age lady guru with rings on every finger, a pierced nose, a flowing robe with half-moons on it and a conical hat. But she was neither. Dr. Field was an extremely attractive, tastefully dressed woman with a lovely smile and a confident but comforting manner. As she invited me in, I couldn't help thinking, "What a fox!"

I'd hoped that we'd be able to just get going with the hypnotherapy, instantly attacking the problem and resolving it. Arthur Ellen had wasted no time with me – he cut to the chase fast. But Dr. Field was much more thorough. Most of that first appointment was taken up with background stuff – Dr. Field asking me many questions about myself and my past, writing my responses down in great detail.

Born in Chicago, raised in Venice, California. One brother, one sister. My sister and my father had died within the past couple of years and I was taking care of my aged mother. Raised Roman Catholic, but no longer active. I'd worked for many years as a commercial artist and as a writer of animated cartoons. When I listed a few of my scores of credits for Dr. Field, she seemed very impressed, which frankly surprised me. It always blew me away when people reacted that way. Years earlier a former writing partner had summed up the lack of respect given animation writers in Hollywood. "Being a good cartoon writer," he said, "was like being the best dressed man in Bulgaria." Perhaps I should talk to more people outside the industry.

Toward the end of the hour I was getting pretty impatient. After all, I could've written out all this dossier stuff on a resume. We had only minutes left and Dr. Field hadn't yet gotten around to addressing what I'd come in for, and her time was not cheap. And, since I'd had some success in the past with hypnosis, I was very hopeful and anxious to get down to business. But Dr. Field suddenly switched gears on me. Putting down her clipboard, she asked me bluntly, "How's your love life?"

The fact was it was suffering, and in no small measure because of the stranglehold this weather fear had on me. But I was embarrassed to talk about it, so I blurted out something like, "What do you want to know that for?" – but as soon as the words were out of my mouth, I realized it was hopeless and stupid to sidestep the issue. So I started telling Dr. Field about my lovely lady friend Susan. We seemed compatible in many ways. Susan was also a writer, working for a large advertising agency. And, like me, she'd never been married. There were some differences – Susan was a gorgeous, petite brunette with green eyes. I'm tall, grey and bloodshot. She was also several years younger. We'd been going together for many months. I liked her friends and she liked mine. We'd even talked of getting married. Everything seemed to be going beautifully – until the rains came and I started getting freaky.

I told the doctor how difficult it had become for me to sleep at Susan's place because she had a noisy gutter outside her window that exaggerated the sound of the falling rain. I'd started bringing earplugs over and sleeping with the pillow over my head. And, of course, when your fear antenna goes up, everything else comes down. I was periodically impotent. And I couldn't talk to her about it because I didn't understand it myself. How do you tell a grown woman you get terrified when rain starts to fall? Add to that the fact that Susan was a very strong-minded person who would rather have hot coals put under her nails than ever consult a psychotherapist. I feared that my admission of this nutty phobia would really hurt if not destroy our relationship.

Dr. Field's big grandfather clock struck six and my time was up. I must admit that I was quite frustrated. I felt we hadn't really gotten anywhere. As she ushered me out of her office, she read my long face and reassured me. "I know you want to get going on this problem, Shawn. I suggest you see me twice a week for a while."

"Twice a week?" I responded, mentally trying to calculate what the cost of all this would be.

"I don't have any doubt that we'll find our way out of your problem, but we'll have to give it everything we've got."

"You mean everything I've got!" I thought to myself as I walked down the corridor toward the exit. I didn't look forward to a protracted series of visits, not just because I was hurting, but because my insurance only paid for a small part of Dr. Field's fee. I seriously considered doubling back to her office and canceling the appointment I'd just made, but when I opened the building's outer door, my mind was quickly changed. It was raining again. Fear once more washed over me like a monsoon. I couldn't wait to return for my next session.

Two days later I was back. More talk and more background. We even got into some of my dreams. Like the one I'd just had the night before.

There had been a rainstorm but it was clearing up. I was trying to return to my house, but I had to get over an enormously high cliff to get there. It was very scary, with mud slides and waterfalls everywhere. But the cliff wasn't just a natural formation. There were treacherous stairs and ladders that I had to climb and leap from one to the other. I was also aware that I was, in effect, taking a shortcut by going up the side of the cliff, instead of taking the long way around it. But it was too late to turn back.

The symbolism was pretty obvious – I was reflecting my desire to get going with solving this problem. But was examining this kind of thing in therapy going to cure my morbid fear of bad weather? I had strong doubts.

It wasn't until our third appointment that Dr. Field finally decided to use hypnotism. Her technique was to take several minutes going from the top of my head to the tips of my toes, relaxing muscle groups as she took me deeper and deeper into trance. She guided me back to a painful childhood experience – I must've been only a toddler. I was supposed to be taking a nap, but I'd gotten out of my bed, gone into the kitchen and spilled a bottle of ammonia. My mother was furious and whacked me hard on the butt. She put me back to bed and gave me a "Wait till your father gets home – he's really going to give it to you" message. This was a frequent theme in my childhood – being threatened by the return home of my dad. I don't remember his ever physically hurting me. But just a disappointed expression on his face was enough to make me feel about as awful as a kid could feel.

One thing I must say here about what I encounter under hypnosis. Some people describe a sense of detachment while in trance – as if they were watching a movie. For me it's a total experience. In this hypnotic incident, I WAS a child. I felt as a child. I could smell the ammonia fumes. I felt the sting of my mother's hand on my bottom. Even my point of view was a child's, seeing everything from a lower angle and much larger than an adult would.

Dr. Field brought me back to consciousness. "Shawn, you're an outstanding hypnotic subject," she enthused.

I didn't respond right away. Coming out of trance for me is like pulling myself out of a tub full of taffy. It took me several minutes to reply. "That's fine," I mumbled with a thick tongue. "But what does this mean? What does spilling a bottle of ammonia have to do with my weather hangup?" Since the hour was up, Dr. Field suggested we get into that next time.

The following couple of appointments we speculated about "the ammonia thing" as well as groping around in my head for

what was behind my fear. Dr. Field had me free associate – trying to get a hook on something, anything that would get us to the
cause. Nothing led anywhere. I was once more hypnotically
regressed to early childhood and re-experienced being tied to a
tree by my mother, so I wouldn't wander off. Again, pretty
unpleasant. But, I thought, also pretty irrelevant. By early
December I'd had three more hypnotic sessions, all having to do
with childhood experiences, none of which seemed to have even
a remote connection to why I'd entered therapy. And since the
weather continued rainy my anxiety was getting worse. I seriously started thinking about looking elsewhere for help.

But a couple of weeks before Christmas we hit a raw nerve.
Dr. Field led me back a few years to re-experience the flood con-
ditions of 1979-80 mentioned earlier. I relived my house being
flooded, my roof leaking and my swimming pool overflowing.
Pretty awful. When I became quite agitated, racing around in my
head filling sandbags to keep the water out, Dr. Field brought me
out of that scene and took me back to still another childhood
experience – I was two years old and hiding under some steps.
It was getting dark and my sister was calling me. Leaves were
blowing outside and the wind was howling. I was scared of being
punished (for what I don't know) but also frightened at being in
this confined, dark place. As the wind picked up and its howling
sound got louder, I grew more and more terrified. I started to
scream and cry uncontrollably.

I was so shaken when Dr. Field brought me out of trance that
after I left her office, I couldn't drive my car. I had to come back
to her waiting room and stay for nearly an hour before I got hold
of myself.

Now I wanted to quit more than ever. But by the time I arrived
home I had to admit to myself that we'd made some kind of a
connection. We hadn't just dredged up some unpleasant old
memories here. The rain, the wind, a frightened child – this
seemed like a definite link between the fears of today and the
events of other times.

All through the rest of December on through early March, I
was close to going over the edge. As the rain and wind continued relentlessly, day after day, I had the most anxious moments

and the darkest thoughts of my entire life. But I continued to see Dr. Field because I felt, hoped and prayed that sooner or later this process was going to lead to relief. My attitude was like the drunk in the old joke, on his hands and knees under a street light. A cop asks him what he's doing there and the drunk replies, "Looking for my keys. I lost 'em across the street." The cop asks, "Then what're you looking here for?" The drunk replies, "Because the light's better."

Through hypnosis, Dr. Field was throwing a lot of light on my forgotten childhood, but I had no idea if we were looking in the right place. In session after session Dr. Field would take me hypnotically to my buried past, and I would relive things like being on a Chicago elevated train station in mid-winter and feeling the bitter cold wind whip up through the platform, then being punished for coming home late. Or being left in a baby buggy by my mother, and when it started to rain, trying to crawl out, only to tip it over and spill groceries all over the street. These and other such hypnotic happenings seemed important because they touched on frightening childhood experiences relating to the weather. But bringing them to the surface did little if anything to lessen the severity of my panic attacks. And as the rain continued to fall in record amounts over the following weeks, the only relief I was getting was from the relaxation suggestions Dr. Field gave me on each visit. But the effect of these would wear off rather quickly, and the suggestions I was taught to give myself didn't really work well.

But then in early March, the weather turned mild, and so did my fears of the wind and rain. As spring approached and the sun shown more and more, I began to think I'd turned the corner on terror. My moods brightened at this prospect, and the fact that I wouldn't have to mention seeing a shrink to Susan buoyed my spirits even more.

In mid March, Susan and I flew to Florida to take a Caribbean cruise. Tremendous turbulence followed us all the way to the east coast. This was not a white knuckle flight, it was a red, white and blue knuckle flight – the roughest, scariest one I've ever been on. When we landed in Miami, there were hurricane warnings. Fortunately, we were booked to stay in a hotel that night instead of boarding the ship right away, because during the early morning hours the lower tip of the storm hit shore. We watched its devastating power from our double-pane bedroom window. Even though we were quite safe, I felt the old whammy starting to grab me again. I had to dip into the tranquilizers to get just a little sleep. Early the next day, when the weather cleared, we took a walk outside. There were several overturned mobile homes nearby and debris everywhere. The damage was in the millions.

It took me two or three days on that cruise ship under sunny Caribbean skies to really settle down. At first I felt defeated, as if I'd really slipped backward. But when we hooked up with friends I'd met on a previous cruise and began to share with them and others the terrible fears that we all felt during the hurricane, I stopped beating on myself for having what was, after all, a normal reaction to real danger. The rest of our vacation was wonderful. Susan and I had a marvelous time, and when we got back home, I felt we'd gotten closer than we'd been for a long while.

I had the last of this series of appointments with Dr. Field on April 13. Refreshed from our trip, I was very optimistic that my weather angst was behind me. Of course I was in denial big time. After all, the rainy season in Southern California was over and I wouldn't have to test myself for at least six months. Dr. Field tried to persuade me to continue my therapy, but I stubbornly refused. As far as I was concerned, I was all better. Sure I was.

In June my mother passed away of a stroke. She was eighty-four years old. I'd been taking care of her for almost three years since my father's death. She'd been in poor health for some time. Losing her was extremely sad and a big loss to me, but not unexpected. Even so, I grieved for quite a long time.

As spring turned to summer the pain of her passing began to subside. I was working on a new cartoon series that was a lot of fun, and Susan and I were getting along well. In September, we flew to Wisconsin to visit my friends Ted and Sue, the couple we'd seen on our cruise. We spent several days at their lake home and had a delightful time. When we got back Susan and I again spoke about getting married. I felt very positive – work was going well for both of us and my weather fears seemed a distant memory. But then in late October, my hibernating terror awoke and struck me with a vengeance. Santana winds came up, fanning brush fires all over Southern California. I was not in a fire area and was not in any imminent danger. But something deep inside me sensed things quite differently. Just the sound of the hot "devil wind" rekindled a feeling of being severely threatened. I was once again in a state of constant panic, right back where I'd been months earlier. All I wanted to do was close the blinds, plug my ears and put a pillow over my head. I started making excuses to stay home and avoid people, including Susan – especially Susan. Needless to say, our relationship quickly began to fall apart. I tried to fake my way through it, but trying to conceal these feelings was like trying to hide an elephant in a shoe box. She was in no mood to put up with my bizarre behavior anymore and started to avoid me. I couldn't blame her. I didn't even want to be around me.

So I went back to Dr. Field. I saw her seven times between November 20 and December 14. Sad to say, things went from bad to worse. On November 23 she took me back to a childhood incident in which I was playing with matches and set a grass fire. On the 30th, I went so deep into trance that I had great difficulty coming out. Quoting my diary, on December 2, "I once more descended into the muddy depths of helplessness." Dr. Field suggested I buy a red sweater and anchor the power of the color red to my dreadful feelings until more good feelings emerged. On Dec. 7, I cried tears of futility because we were again raking over old coals but going nowhere. On Dec. 9, she told me it was okay that I felt bad when I left her office. "Feelings are significant and need to be experienced as they are felt," she declared. "Like a kitchen sink, if we shove the debris down, eventually the drain gets clogged," she told me. "That leads to anxiety and even panic attacks." On December 14, Dr. Field and I had a very testy exchange. I complained loudly that we weren't getting anyplace. I told her it just pissed me off for her to tell me to wear red sweaters and accept bad feelings. On the 21st, we once again had what I felt was a very unproductive session.

Meantime, a few days before Christmas, Susan and I had a terrible row. I tried to tell her about going to therapy and got an

even harsher response than I'd always feared. She had no toler-
ance for the process and thought my problem was trivial. There
were other very personal and very unkind remarks. I was
crushed. A couple of days later she apologized, saying she'd been
worried about having cancer which she now knew she didn't
have. I don't know if that was just an excuse or not, but as far as
I was concerned it was another hole in our fast sinking rowboat
of love.

It didn't rain on December 23, 1993, but it was to be a water-
shed. It had been very breezy all day, and I hadn't been able to
concentrate on the script I was writing. I was anxious about the
wind and depressed about my troubles with Susan. And I was
angry – at myself and at Dr. Field for our mutual inability to free
me from the clutches of my weather mania. As I entered the
doctor's office, I was aching for a breakthrough. But I had no
idea of the dramatic form it would take.

from...Dr. Field
The Therapist's Perspective

"The soul should always stand ajar,
ready to welcome the ecstatic experience."
—Emily Dickinson

"In the twilight of memory we should meet once more,
we shall speak again together,
and you shall sing to me a deeper song.
Know therefore, that from the greater silence I shall return."
—Kahlil Gibran, *The Prophet*

Twisting and turning in the deep leather of the patient's chair, his face turned into a terrified grimace. Shattering the still quiet of the office, he jolted my concentration with a loud piercing scream which could only emanate from someone's experiencing severe pain. Shawn was in a hypnotic trance. I did not need to ascertain that he was into some traumatic episode – he was definitely there! But where?

"Really get with that feeling," I urged. "Put aside whatever is going on in your head for the moment and focus upon the physical sensations you are experiencing, the physical feelings." He did not speak, and, as if still feeling the pain, he contorted his face and continued to writhe in the chair. He was totally within himself and I could not tell whether he was concentrating upon the feelings or simply had not heard me. Or, what in heaven's name was going on?

"Are you more than five years old?" I questioned. "Let a 'Yes' finger lift." We joke about giving someone the finger, but here's where the patient gives the therapist the finger. Utilized in regression therapy, the patient responds directly from the subconscious by lifting a finger designated as, "Yes", "No", or "I don't want to tell you". Any bodily movements come from the subconscious mind. In contrast, when a subject needs to provide a verbal response, he needs to *think*. The response is then more apt to come from the conscious mind. Working with the fingers is like working with the Ouija Board. One might say, "Let the fingers do the talking."

Shawn and I had reviewed many past events in his life and he was an old hand at providing worthwhile responses. In fact, his fingers probably danced in his dreams. Yet, there were absolutely no finger responses now. This was not typical of my psychotherapy sessions with him.

As we began this session, little did either of us suspect that it would be the one to produce the key we had been looking for – and to bring it about in such a surprising manner. Indeed, we had not set out to do any regression therapy at all. Shawn came into the session complaining about an intense pain in his chest. Prior to coming to my office, Shawn had consulted with his physician who determined there was no serious physical condition. With this assurance, we agreed to spend the time of his hour doing pain management to provide him with some relief. With a hypnotic induction, powerful mind-over-body control can be invoked within which the patient *removes* the pain. Actually, the relay system to the brain is *cut off*, so that even if profound tissue damage is present, the pain is not felt.

So, with Shawn's permission to be touched, and after providing Mesmeric passes with my hands gliding about six inches over his body, I moved my fingers lightly over his chest where the pain was most intense. As I did, I again requested that he really "pay attention" to the pain and focus upon the physical sensations of which the pain was comprised. And then it happened!

This handsome guy — tall, dark, and stately — had returned to me for therapy one month earlier. When he had begun treatment one year prior, my initial impression was that of a man with a very quiet demeanor and impeccable manners, such as never taking his seat until I placed my derriere on mine. His presenting symptoms, a fear of wind, rain, or actually any gloomy weather, resulted in a level of panic which was overwhelming to him. This produced a depressive mood which I believe was reflected in his attire, mostly black, with some grey. Boris, my office manager, observed that after his session, Shawn would sometimes go to the parking lot exit, look out through the glass doors, and if it were at all gloomy, come back to the waiting room and sit shivering until he could desperately create enough courage to deal with the elements and venture out to his car.

In therapy, Shawn turned out to be a "tough nut to crack". I pride myself on "getting rid of my patients fast". These actually have been the words of some of my patients. Medical hypnosis is a powerful tool of psychotherapy, greatly accelerating the process. Not with Shawn. Every form of psychotherapy and hypnotherapy in which I was skilled was put to the test with only minimal returns. Exploring the past, we worked through every rainy, windy, or watery episode he could come up with, looking to find the key to the door behind which resided the causative factors to his symptoms. Once there, with some unique hypnotic interventions and a "working through", with the release of the feelings which were a part of these events, the causative factors could be defused or sometimes re-framed into a positive situation.

Yes, I could not have been more surprised and amazed. No response came from Shawn as to where, when, or what he was about. Having been in private practice for twenty years, I had never had such a reaction from a motivated patient. No response! Yet there were the sighs of anguish and pain and the twisting and turning in the chair. "Are you at home? School? Is your mother there? Sister?" I kept questioning. Still no response.

Barely audible, Shawn finally muttered, "It's 1917." What? I was totally taken aback. 1917? Wait a minute. He's not nearly that old. He must mean "1970". Then he blurted out, "I'm in the trenches... France... Or Belgium." He said nothing more until much time passed. I waited and listened for additional information. Then, maybe he was out of trance, or maybe we were both in a lingering light trance. We talked. "It was *The* World War," he declared in all innocence. His aspect was still a bit fuzzy. "Oh! World War I," he corrected, as he became further aware and began to view his experience from another perspective, that of the Self sitting in the chair before me. He was now ready to talk about whatever he could get out of his mouth.

"War... the sounds... the sights... the piercing cold... the terrible, never-ceasing rain... and then, the bayonet... the German soldier... the bloody Kraut... pierced by his damn steel bayonet... He leaped into the trench and he got me... in the chest. He stabbed me in the chest! The son of a bitch! Right in the chest! Oh, the pain! Pain in my chest!" He continued to cry out. Thus began the unraveling of an unforeseen saga, and with it, the beginning of an even more amazing recovery! Similar to what the drunk in Shawn's little tale had to say, the light was on this side of the room, but the "key" had indeed been "across the street".

II

In "The" War

II

IN "THE" WAR

r. Field had her hands full trying to bring me back from my horror-stricken state. I was hysterical. I really thought I'd experienced what it's like to be killed. My face was bathed in tears and I could feel cold sweat soaking through my shirt. After many soothing suggestions, several tissues and a glass of water, I was able to relax enough to start telling Dr. Field the details of what had just happened – being in the French countryside during World War I, the unspeakable dampness and bone chilling cold, the riveting vividness of the sounds, sights and smells of the battlefield, and ultimately the sickening sensation of possibly being stabbed to death. If one picture is worth a thousand words, one trance experience like this increased the word count a hundredfold.

So much had been packed into that brief hypnotic happening that I went way over my allotted time attempting to give Dr. Field the full story. She was amazed as I was at this completely unsolicited leap backward into another time's terror. What did it mean? Was it a genuine past-life experience or just my imagination, supercharged by the hypnotic state? And what did it have to do with my present day phobia? Unfortunately for me, Dr. Field's backed-up schedule did not permit us to search for any more pieces to my puzzle that day. But we both expressed our desire to delve deeper at my next appointment. As I left her office, I got some peculiar looks from the two patients who were sitting in the waiting room. I wondered if it were just because I'd eaten into their time or if my face looked as befuddled as I felt.

That image of the German soldier stabbing me with his bayonet kept coming back to me as I drove home. I was so preoccupied that I made a couple of really stupid moves behind the wheel, changing lanes without looking, almost sideswiping a pickup truck, and making an unsafe left turn into the teeth of oncoming traffic. The second close call shook the picture of the menacing German soldier out of my head, but I couldn't get rid of the stabbing sensation in my chest. I thought of going directly to my doctor, but that was ridiculous. I'd already seen him about it. Just a bunch of crazy mind games. It's the hypnosis – it can cause all kinds of hell when you screw around with the unconscious. Got to put all this b.s. out of my head. So I tuned my car radio to the most raucous rock station I could find, turned up the volume full blast and boogied the rest of the way home.

By the time I pulled into my driveway it was getting dark. Almost every house on my block was aglow with holiday lights. It was a cheery picture. And, the sensation in my chest had been downgraded from a stab to a poke. I got in the door, scooped up a pile of cards the postman had deposited through my mail chute and went through them quickly before hefting a stack of presents I'd purchased and headed out the door again. Susan had invited me over for Christmas Eve dinner. As I pulled onto the freeway, headed for her condo in West Hollywood, the sensation in my chest grew stronger again. I tried to put it out of my mind with an overlay of other thoughts, like my favorite distraction – baseball statistics. I'm a kind of nut on the subject. I started quizzing myself – What did Heinie Manush bat in 1937? Who hit more home runs, Mike Schmidt or Mickey Mantle? What year did they move the pitcher's rubber from fifty feet away from home plate to sixty feet, six inches? How many outfielders can I think of whose first name is Bob?

I was still mentally asking myself questions like these when I was greeted by Susan at her door. She looked the picture of Christmas in her fuzzy white angora sweater and bright red skirt. We were both full of smiles and small talk as we placed gifts under her tree and then sat down to dinner. I thought I'd at last put the bayonet blues away for the night, but I guess I unconsciously kept rubbing my ribs because Susan commented on it at dinner. I brushed it off, but for the next couple of hours my head was off in some other place, and not in my mental baseball record book either. It was just as well that Susan had a small project from work she had to finish after we ate, because I was not much more fun than a temporary filling. We went to bed early and again, as I tried to sleep, there was that image and that damned pain back again.

Christmas day was bright and sunny. I had all but forgotten the German soldier with his bayonet and the sensation in my chest was at last gone. We awoke and quickly got into the yuletide spirit, exchanging our gifts. Susan beamed at the Gucci watch bracelet I gave her and I was overwhelmed by the sheer number of presents she gave me – among them, a beautiful leather jacket, as well as a watch and some studs. Like little kids, we spontaneously broke into a chorus of "Rudolf, the Red Nosed Reindeer" as we ate a big breakfast. Then we left to drop in on her friends, Eddie and May before coming back to her place where several members of her family were due. More gifts were exchanged before we put away a huge Christmas dinner. For the first time since my hypnotic encounter with death I was feeling great.

The next couple of days the weather continued to be beautiful, so naturally my woes slipped into the background. I got back to work on a new cartoon script and made a visit to my gym to try to work off the after-effects of all the Christmas gluttony. But on Tuesday, Dec. 28, the "insanity", as I called it, started all over again. I saw Dr. Field to report how much better I felt. We chatted amiably for a while about what we'd done over the holidays before getting down to business. If anything, Dr. Field was even more interested than I was in the very bizarre experience we'd shared a few days earlier. What was it all about? She'd never seen anything quite like it in all her years as a hypnotherapist – none of her patients had ever spontaneously reverted to another life. As anxious as she was to go back again and explore further, that's how reluctant I was. After all, it had been one of the most unpleasant experiences of my life. Returning to that scene was like volunteering for my own execution. But when Dr. Field convinced me of how important it might be to get at the heart of my problem, I allowed her to put me under.

It didn't take her long to guide me back into that vast unexplored inner world of my mind. She had me close my eyes and relax my muscles, from the top of my head to the tips of my toes. As my body let go of its natural tension, I started to drift into a very pleasant state. Unlike sleep, there was never any loss of awareness while I was in a hypnotic trance induced by Dr. Field. No matter how deep I went, I was still able to hear her voice and have a sense of connectedness to where my body was. And yet, my mind was streaking back in time – into ANOTHER time – a time I, as Shawn Regan, had never experienced. Suddenly the pleasant feelings changed to a sense of foreboding. I began to breathe deeper and deeper and to feel terribly cold as I suddenly took on another identity.

"Ugh! This bloody awful rain!" I grumbled.

"Who am I speaking to?" Dr. Field inquired.

"Lance Corporal John H. WIlliams!" I snapped, as if replying to some senior officer. I was shivering almost uncontrollably.

"Where are you, John?" Dr. Field asked.

I couldn't reply right away. All I could do was wrap my arms around my torso and move my legs back and forth. The piercing sense of damp cold was almost overwhelming. Then a sudden bolt of lightning lit up the world around me.

"I'm in France."

"What's the date?"

"M-march... nineteen s-s-sixteen," I stammered.

"A year earlier than the last time we talked?"

I nodded yes. I could see the dark gray clouds and hear the rain pelting down on my helmet. In the distance, the sounds of shells exploding were reverberating through the air. I was marching in full battle gear along with many other British soldiers through a marshy field. There was a rotten smell everywhere – I couldn't tell where it was coming from – the slime underfoot or maybe from the bandaged arm of the soldier in front of me or, who knows, maybe it was from my own mildewed uniform. I gripped the stock of my rifle with numb fingers as I slogged along through the heavy mud. My aching, blistered feet slid around inside my boots. I was wearing a slicker, but I might as well have been naked because I couldn't possibly have felt more soaked through.

As I tried to verbalize this vision of misery through chattering teeth, my distorted sense of time only added to the awfulness. It seemed like I marched on for hours, but of course it was only a few minutes. After I fell a couple of times from pure exhaustion, Dr. Field gave me the suggestion that I'd reached my destination. Now it was night. I found myself inside a tent. But there was no getting away from the incessant rain. It continued to pour down, seeping in under the canvas and splashing through the wavering door flap as the wind blew harder and harder. There I was, sitting in mud, not caring whether I lived or died – the most wonderful thing in the world would've been simply to get dry.

While I huddled in this hovel, I pulled a hunk of stale bread out of my backpack and began to chew on it. Like everything else, it was moldy. I thought of how wonderful it would be to be home in England with my young wife.

"What's your wife's name, John?" Dr. Field asked.

"Maggie."

I apparently smiled because Dr. Field asked me why I suddenly looked so pleased. "I can just see her in the kitchen bringing me a steaming bowl of stew and a pint. We just tied the knot before I come over. Haven't seen her for over a year."

"Where is home?"

"We live in London but she's staying with her mum in Leeds while I'm off playing soldier."

I went silent for a time as I thought of my lovely young bride. I could see her pale green eyes and the copper colored highlights in her long, wavy, auburn hair. Then I was suddenly back in the cold and damp of my tent. I began to sob.

"What's the matter, John?" asked Dr. Field.

"It's no use – I'll never come back from this stinking war. It's bloody hopeless. It's not going to end until every man-Jack of us is blown to hell." Then I started to laugh.

"What's funny?"

"I just thought – 'Blown to hell!' Ha! I wish they would blow me to hell – at least it doesn't rain there."

"How do you know it doesn't rain in hell?"

"Well, if it rained, that'd put out the fire, wouldn't it?"

I chuckled at my own gallows humor, but then I heard rapid gunfire, like a machine gun. It seemed quite close. The flap of my tent flew open and there was my Sergeant Major telling me we had to clear out. Leave the tent and get moving on the double. Once more I was outside in the rain, running and ducking as bullets whistled through the air, seemingly from every direction. I had no idea where we were going. It was so dark that all I could see were the vague shadowy shapes of my fellow infantrymen as we scrambled through the muddy field, looking for cover. My heart raced as I tried to keep up. Then I tripped over something.

"Oh my God!"

"What is it? What's happening, John?"

"It's a body! I fell over a body! Can't tell if he's ours or theirs! Too dark. Can't stop. Have to leave him, poor devil!"

Once more I was on my feet, stumbling along, hoping to find some place to shield me from the ceaseless gunfire. Then I got all turned around. In the dark, I couldn't see where the rest of my company had gone. I stood there, turning in circles, trying to peer through the inky rain. Suddenly there was someone right next to me. I cried out.

"What's happening, John?" asked the doctor.

"He grabbed me and pulled me to the ground. It's alright – it's the Sergeant Major. He's telling me to stay down. He's got a grenade – he's pulling the pin. He jumps up and throws into the dark, then dives back to the ground. There's an explosion. Now... nothing."

"What do you mean, 'nothing'?"

"I mean the gunfire's stopped. Must've knocked out a Kraut machine gun nest."

The Sergeant Major and I got to our feet and the two of us hightailed it out of there. The war and the rain faded away and I seemed to go into a kind of neutral state. Then, instead of running alongside the sergeant, I was back in England, walking with

Maggie. We were strolling by a riverbank that flowed through a beautiful green glade. It was summertime. Dr. Field asked me a couple of times to describe what was happening, but I didn't feel like responding right away. I just wanted to drink in the warmth of the sun and the sound of the birds and feel Maggie's soft white hand in mine. Dr. Field again asked me what I was experiencing.

"I'm with Maggie. We're standing by our favorite spot near the river."

"Is this before or after the war?"

"During the war. We've just decided to get married. I'm kissing her."

Suddenly we were no longer by the river.

"You're scowling. What's the matter?"

"We're at the train station. Lots of people around. I'm in uniform. I'm kissing Maggie goodbye. She says to be careful and come back soon. I tell her not to worry. It'll all be over in three months and we'll be back together again. I want to believe it, but deep down I know it's the bull. She says she'll write to me every day. I kiss her again and get on the train. It's pulling out and I'm waving to her. She's running along and waving back. Oh, I've got this terrible feeling I'll never see her again. Oh, God, no! I'm back!"

"Back home?"

"No. In that bloody trench. Just like last time – my gun's jammed. I know that son of a bitch with the bayonet is going to get me! I know it!"

Dr. Field now assured me that I didn't have to re-experience the wound as before. I could view everything as I would on a theater screen. She promised there would be no pain. She was right. I saw the whole thing again, but as if it were happening in slow motion to someone else. The German soldier dived into the trench and speared me. He was instantly shot dead by the soldier beside me. Then, like a movie ending, everything went to black. But after a few seconds, I felt my body being buffeted about.

"Why are you jerking around like that, John?" Dr. Field asked. I couldn't answer her – not just because I didn't know, but because my mouth wouldn't work. Then I heard a siren blaring. I smelled exhaust fumes. I opened my eyes and saw someone working over me. He was bandaging my chest.

"John, where are you?" the doctor asked for the third or fourth time.

"I'm in a truck!" I was finally able to say. "I'm in a truck – and I'm alive!"

From the Therapist's Perspective

*"The big question is whether you are going to be able
to say a hearty yes to your adventure."*
—Joseph Campbell

During my years of private practice, I have guided many patients in a trance state over distant journeys by way of age regression. In age regression, the patient is asked to return to an earlier time in his life when the causative factor or the *key* to a particular trauma began. Combined with psychotherapy, hypnotherapy produces incredible results. The turnabout in these patients' lives has often been awesome, but none had ever slipped into a past life adventure. Furthermore, that day, my intent was to ultimately get to pain management; we were not even going to employ age regression, which we indeed had used many times before.

I had never given any credence to past life therapy. The whole situation hit me like a dinosaur-sized rock. When I left my office that evening, what Shawn had encountered in that session created turmoil in my mind, a turning upside-down of my own once held theories and beliefs developed over years of experience in medical hypnosis. My peers in the American Society of Clinical Hypnosis and its component section, the Los Angeles Academy of Clinical Hypnosis, did not give credence to Past Life Therapy. So what was I to think? That which had transpired also touched on my personal religious beliefs which do not include the concept of reincarnation, except for the symbolic resurrection of the soul. However, need I now explore the mysticism associated with the Kabbalah, a part of the Hassidic tradition?

My brain was churning with thoughts. Could that event to which Shawn returned have some bearing on his behavior today? Was there more to that story? If we backtracked to that time again, would it yield some answers we'd been seeking for nine months? What triggered his spontaneous regression to the past life? Did it have anything to do with the pain he had when he walked into the office? At that point, I did not begin to envisage the saga which would unfold and its impact on both our lives. Shawn would not only return to that scenario, but, bit by bit, this completely different person in a completely different time and place would continue to emerge and have an awesome effect upon Shawn's life today.

I had a gut feeling that we had really hit on something which was going to shed incredible light on Shawn's situation. It reminded me of what one of my doctoral professors had once said — that I had some psychic qualities about me which would be of benefit to me as a therapist. I'd laughed it off in the 70's, but here was a real test in the 90's. Before our next session, I began reviewing past life therapy in books, medical journals, and seminar recordings I had on hand. I'd been through them before and passed them off as interesting but not applicable to my practice. Now I found them to be fascinating reading, increasing my excitement to continue this direction in the therapy.

I also thought about the hippocampus, a pea-sized portion of the brain, which is our bank of long range memories. It contains so much data that I imagine it to be the size of that ungainly creature, the hippopotamus. These memories can be brought to the surface — and we can be most amazed, when suddenly we recall information we had not thought about in years. All these memories are intact and can be retrieved by associations, dreams and especially by way of hypnosis. *But does this area of the brain contain knowledge of experiences prior to birth?*

My late friend and mentor, David Cheek, M.D., OB-GYN and past president of the American Society of Clinical Hypnosis, researched information stored in the brain while in the womb. He also observed the influence on present behavior of birth experiences, such as a mother's attitude, bonding between the newborn and mother, a father's presence, the behavior of the doctor and nurses at the time of the delivery, and which body part emerged first. But what about memories before the embryo evolved? Can memories of an earlier life really exist?

Carl Jung, psychiatrist, spoke of a "collective unconscious" whereby one is born with a common knowledge of all ancestors and cultures which have made up the universe since time immemorial. There are also other theories such as the "Morphic

Resonance" theory of Rupert Sheldrake which implies a universal field of memory to which everyone has access. But such theories certainly do not account for the memory of one person, like Shawn, for a character from out of the past, like John, that causes such turmoil for Shawn Regan.

What impressed me more than anything were the publications of Dr. Ian Stevenson, the well respected Professor of Psychiatry at the University of Virginia and author of *Children Who Experience Previous Lives.* Dr. Stevenson had researched the memories of children who could speak a foreign language but had never, in this life, been exposed to that language. This phenomenon is referred to as "xenoglossy". Others have also reported stories of children who "remember" the names of people from past lives and can talk about them. Surprisingly, put to the test, much of what these children had said was substantiated.

Psychiatrist Brian Weiss's book, *Many Lives, Many Masters* relates many fragmented episodes from the past lives of his patient, Catherine, which ultimately freed her from the numerous phobias and anxieties from which she had suffered. In *Reincarnation and Biology,* Stevenson reports on birthmarks, blemishes, and irregularities in persons, which correspond to entrance or exit holes of bullets that put an end to "that" person in a past life. He believes that the unique appearances in these individuals are his strongest reason for believing in reincarnation. Dr. Robert Jarman, psychiatrist, and author of *Discovering the Soul,* refers to past life therapy as *spiritual healing.* One recovers the soul and heals it. Like I, he sees "regression therapy" as "total healing" in the sense that we are working with the complete human being — *mind, body and soul.*

As I continued my research, assessment, and contemplation of Shawn, I was glowing with excitement and curiosity concerning what would come up next. Feeling like I had landed on a planet I had known about before but had no intrigue to explore, I could not now leave and return home. Then the thought came to me — what if Shawn does not want to pursue the past life? My excitement turned to trepidation. Shoving what I believe he "should" do down a patient's throat is not in my bag of tricks. My technique is to take the patient from *where he is at.* This is appropriate and is supported by ethical considerations. In practice, when I believe a certain approach to be in order, such as performing an age regression or mind-body control for pain management, I suggest the process and then get the patient's permission to proceed. After the patient is in a trance state, I direct a further question to the subconscious, "Would it be alright to learn more about your...?" Filled with my own apprehension as to whether Shawn would be amenable to continuing the past life regressions, and the numerous questions to be resolved if he did, the time between sessions with Shawn seemed to drag on interminably.

My grandfather clock chimed five PM and there was Shawn sitting in the waiting room, ready for his session. After chit-chatting a bit about holiday happenings, we got into his unexpected voyage into the past — and more about his last session. Shawn had questions, and so did I. "Could it be real?" "Was it true?" "Is it valid?" Neither of us had the answers. Then, I asked the inevitable question; "Do you think you might like to return to that experience?"

Perhaps my own enthusiasm carried me beyond the point where I usually go to encourage a patient. I did my best to temper my excitement. But somehow my inner vibes were right out there in front. I knew Shawn picked it up and I had mixed feelings about that. Based on the traumatic aspect of the past life experience, he was obviously hesitant to return to it. Still, I detected an inner desire on his part to continue the journey. I did not push; I did encourage. On the theory that the return to this past life might reveal some information to hasten his recovery, Shawn agreed to go for it.

Shawn is an excellent hypnosis subject. Accompanied by some Mesmeric energy passes, with my hands gliding about six inches over his body, I did a progressive relaxation induction with him, a process whereby one relaxes in sequence each part of the body. Within a few seconds, Shawn slipped into hypnosis and immediately went back to that past life, complaining about the "bloody rain" in a voice tinged with both an English accent and an Irish brogue. I asked with whom I was speaking and received an abrupt reply, "Lance Corporal John Williams". This was accompanied by a back and forward movement of his legs on the hassock. Also, his body was quivering.

He was experiencing the events mentioned earlier – marching endlessly in the "dreadful rain", with the sounds and smell of war all around him. Then, delightful memories of being with his lovely wife changed the picture to one of warmth and pleasure. The description of the closeness between him and Maggie engulfed me; it was so vivid. That aura was short-lived as he was suddenly back in the horror of the war again.

His experience of the feelings associated with the stabbing incident was clearly an excruciatingly painful trauma for him. Therefore, I chose to move on to an alternative approach, allowing him to step back from the trauma, viewing it from a distance in what is called a "Three Part Dissociation". In this technique, the patient divides into three ego states or Selves. Part of the patient, one of the Selves, is in a projection booth in a movie house and is looking down at himself seated in the theater. The Self sitting in the theater is, in turn, watching the movie screen where his "Younger Self", or Self from the Past, is going through the traumatic experience for the very last time. Utilization of the Three Part Dissociation allows the patient to go through the traumatic experience with no damage to his ego. The Self from the Past goes through the trauma for the present Self.

With Shawn, I suggested the Younger Self be seen as the Self from the past life. And that Self would experience the trauma of being wounded by the bayonet *for the very last time*. Shawn observed the episode from a distance and avoided being over-whelmed once more by the dreadful feelings which he had already experienced intensely. As I called upon both Shawn from this life, and John from the past life, the dialogue went like this:

> Shawn, I'd like a part of you to float out behind you and into the projection booth of a theater. We shall call that part of you 'The Watching Self'. That Watching Self will watch you, sitting in the theater in a seat next to me. You have all the strength of your adult manhood plus the additional strength and support I offer you by my hand holding yours (I took a strong hold on his left hand, the side closest to me). In a moment, not just yet, we'll see the Self from the Past, John, on the movie screen, going through that

dreadful experience for you — being pierced by that bayonet — this time and for the very last time. Shawn, see John for the moment, in a still shot now, way out there before you on the movie screen.

Do you understand the directions? Good! Then run that film now: Your Watching Self in the projection booth is now watching you and me sitting in the theater, in turn, watching John on that movie screen going through that dreadful trauma this time and for the very last time. Let that Self on the screen — your Self from the Past — feel the awful feelings for you now — really have him feel those feelings intensely— so intensely — that both of you can fully let go of those feelings. Let him feel those feelings for you strongly, feel those feelings this time and for the very last time. Meanwhile, should you wish, You, the Self in the chair, can now experience some feelings for him also, should you wish.

When I observed by way of his body language that Shawn had completed watching this movie, I then stated:

Now Shawn, I would like you to reach out with both arms in front of you (I guided his hands) and bring that Past Self back into your body, for after all, as we are discovering, he is a part of you. Hold him close, love him, embrace him, and assure him that you are his Self from the future, and that all is OK. Assure him that He managed to survive that terrible incident and that He will be alright. Hug him tightly and continue to reassure him.

The Three Part Dissociation worked well, as Shawn reviewed the episode from a distance and avoided becoming overwhelmed by the dreadful feelings which he had already experienced. With this technique, he "went through" this episode "for the very last time".

John now saw himself on the way to the hospital with his chest being bandaged — **grateful to be very much alive.**

III

The
Homecoming

III

THE HOMECOMING

*W*hen Dr. Field brought me back to the waking state, my head was in the here-and-now but my feelings were still somewhere in that awful past. I was shivering with cold and continued to suffer chills as we went over what I'd just been through. Dr. Field tried to get me to warm up with suggestions, but without success. She finally brewed me a cup of hot tea and that helped to melt away my frosty hangover.

To say that I was profoundly shaken by this frightening experience is like saying that King Kong is a trifle oversized. It all seemed so vivid, so real, and yet the question remained: was it something that had actually happened in another incarnation or was I just dramatizing, making a wide screen feature film about my fear of foul weather?

If it were just some psycho-production, why did I make up such a character and situation? How did my life as Shawn Regan relate in any way to an English soldier in World War I? I have no English blood and the only military service I ever had was two years of Air Force R.O.T.C.. And yet I must admit that on my two brief visits to England as a tourist I had an eery sense of familiarity about the place, particularly London. I also have what some might call an inordinate fondness for English things – especially their theater and their sense of humor. I'd much rather see an old Alec Guinness movie or hear a Noel Coward song than watch the latest car chase flick from Hollywood or listen to any of the Top Forty. I have no idea where these preferences come from. I was brought up on baseball, hot dogs, apple pie and Chevrolets. Even so, this vacuum cleaner we call the human mind is constantly sucking in all sorts of random information. Who can tell what kind of scenario the hypnotized subconscious will arrange from these miscellaneous pieces of knowledge?

On the other hand, what would it really mean if I, as another person, had actually had these experiences? Until this time, I'd never given the subject of reincarnation much attention. I tended to think it was just self-deception by people with dull little lives, fantasizing that they'd once been Napoleon or Julius Caesar or Cleopatra in order to cloak themselves with a false mantle of self-importance. But if that were the case, why wouldn't I have recreated myself as Mozart or George Washington or Babe Ruth? Who needed to be an obscure soldier with a war wound?

Dr. Field had an open mind on the subject of whether my past-life as John Williams was indeed genuine, but true or not, she felt I'd made a big breakthrough and encouraged me to meditate on this "other life" on my own time. Now that the top was off my mental toothpaste tube, maybe I could squeeze out some more vital information. As I left her office I told her I'd give it a try. But I had second thoughts as I drove home. These mental junkets back to other times and places in another man's persona had a very disturbing effect on me. Peeling back the surface of my unconscious was exposing a lot of raw nerve tissue. Instead of releasing any anxiety I had about wind and rain, I felt even more uneasy, even though the weather continued clear and mild. Who could tell how I'd react to a full blown storm now?

Later that afternoon I brought my boss the finished script I'd been writing. I had worked for one of the major animation production companies for many years. I wrote and edited everything from six minute shorts to feature length films and considered myself very lucky to be able to do what I loved for a living.

Even so, script meetings can sometimes be miserable experiences, especially when you're working with an editor or a network executive who isn't really sure of himself or herself. Quite often that kind of person will want to make changes just for the sake of change. But with my boss, whom many, including myself, considered a creative cartoon genius, there was never any of that. Our story conferences were always pure fun and never seemed like work.

That day, however, I made a real chore out of it for myself because I was so distracted by images of the horrors of a long ago war. I know I made some very puzzling remarks as I lost track of what we were doing a few times. Luckily there wasn't much to change in my script, so I don't think I came across as too deranged, at least not any more than the average cartoon writer.

I had planned to see Susan that night, but she wasn't feeling well, so I stayed home and watched TV. But all the sitcoms in the world couldn't get that John Williams character out of my mind. Finally I decided that if I can't lick him, maybe I'd join him again. I turned off the set, put my feet up and gave myself the same sequenced relaxation suggestions that Dr. Field used on me. I told myself that my mind would slowly drift back over time – not censoring anything, just letting thoughts come, staying as long as they liked, then exiting for something else – familiar things at first, snatches of daily activities, a few childhood memories, then a kind of pleasant gray state – almost falling asleep.

Now unfamiliar things started popping into my mind, like looking into a mirror, but instead of seeing my own reflection, I saw a very slender young man in his twenties with slicked down red hair and a shaggy mustache. He was shaving with a straight razor and lather, something I never did. Then I saw this young man moving down a street full of shops. It looked like London. He stopped in front of one place, put a key in the lock and opened the door. I got a whiff of leather. I saw men's shoes displayed on a counter. This was his business – a shoe shop – an upscale establishment where boots were made to order for well-to-do clients.

Then I was in a pub. A very jolly, earthy barmaid handed me a large drink. It seemed like we were great friends. I sat down at a piano and began to play. Others started singing along. I drifted off to sleep after that.

The next morning, I awoke feeling much better than I had the previous day. The gloom and doom that had followed me around was gone, there were no clouds on the horizon and the images dredged up from yesteryear were for the moment back in the past. The rest of the day was quite pleasant. I had a delightful lunch with a few of the other fellows from the studio. We talked a lot of cartoon biz gossip and had a lot of laughs. As always, everyone was full of "put-down" jokes, telling one after another on each-other. For the second straight night I didn't see Susan. She was still not feeling well, at least, that was what she said. I worried that, rather than actually being physically ill, she was just sick of me. It's not a good idea to dwell on negative thoughts like this, especially while eating dinner. My stomach growled at me all night.

The following day, December 30, I again saw Dr. Field. It was one of the more remarkable and important hypnotic sessions of all, maybe the most important, because it opened up so much. I let the doctor know I was feeling pretty good – no stabbing pains, no fears, no sense of danger. But the weather had been beautiful, so there hadn't been any chance to test whether what we were doing was having any therapeutic effect. I told her about my own private attempt at self-hypnosis, picking up random bits of information from my unconscious which seemed to be connected to our previous work together. Dr. Field got quite excited about this and suggested we try to put these pieces together with hypnosis. That would have to wait for another time, however, because our John Williams journey was to go off in an unexpected direction.

As I went under, the first thing I experienced was the return of the chest pain – but instead of a stabbing sensation it seemed more spread out across my upper torso. Then a general feeling of malaise came over me – I felt nauseated and weak. I began squirming in my chair.

"Where are you?" asked Dr. Field.

I couldn't tell, at least not yet. Other things came to me: sounds of men groaning and moaning, a feeling of hustle and bustle all about me. Then, putrid smells, battling with the scent of antiseptic. I wasn't describing these things to Dr. Field yet, only sensing them. All my muscles felt strained and achy, as though I'd over-exercised. Once more Dr. Field asked me to tell her where I was. As I twisted and turned, trying to alleviate my extreme discomfort, I began to focus in. The first thing I saw was a red cross. My vision grew clearer and I could tell it was worn by a very pretty young nurse with dark hair, but she wasn't dressed the way nurses dress today. She was wearing a long white dress and one of those funny starched hats that nurses wore years ago. Her apron had stains on it – probably blood. She looked very tired as she adjusted a rubber tube that was going into my chest. I had other tubes in my upper arms. She smiled as she wiped my forehead. I suddenly felt very thirsty.

Once more Dr. Field asked me to tell her where I was. But all I could say was "I want a drink of water. I want a drink of water." The nurse wouldn't give me one – she'd only wet my mouth with a moist towel. She said it wasn't good for me in my condition to drink water.

After a while, I was able to look around and view my surroundings. It was a huge field hospital, possibly a converted hangar. There were men in beds everywhere, as far as the eye could see. Nurses and medics raced around through the narrow passageways between the beds, trying desperately to take care of all these poor devils. The cries and occasional screams of the sick and wounded echoed through the huge wooden building. I tried again to describe all this to Dr. Field, but all I could do for quite some time was to mutter and mumble incoherently.

I was in terrible pain now. I asked the nurse for something to alleviate it. She apologized to me, saying they couldn't give me anything – their supplies of all medicines were running out. I closed my eyes and suddenly the pain left. I was back with Maggie – walking hand in hand in that same glen by the river. We seemed to float along, above the ground. The sun cast its radiant warmth across her face, giving her features an iridescent golden glow. But then I was jerked back to the hospital, once more experiencing the agony. I was bathed in sweat now, but I shuddered with chills. Then Dr. Field's voice broke through.

"You look so agonized. What are you feeling, John?"

My mouth finally worked. "Pain!" I said. "In my chest – and all through my body."

Dr. Field gave me a suggestion that I would feel no more pain. It slowly melted away. I was then able to relate to her much of what I was seeing and experiencing as she questioned me.

"Where is this field hospital located?" she asked.

"We're about twenty kilometers behind the lines. But you can still hear the cannon fire in the distance."

"How long have you been there?"

"The nurse says three or four days."

"Have they told you anything about your wound?"

"No. But I'm going to be alright. I know I'm going to be alright. I've got to be. Have to get back to my Maggie. Oh my God! Will you look at me!"

"What do you mean?"

"I can see myself – like I was looking in a mirror. I look bloody terrible!"

"What do you see – Can you describe yourself?"

"Lord, how thin and pale and sucked in I am. Like a bleedin' spook!" I started to shake again.

"What's happening now, John?"

"There's a horrible draft in this place – the ceiling's so high. And the roof leaks. I think they used to keep aeroplanes in here. Or maybe barrage balloons. Can I get another blanket? I'm that frozen. Damn!"

"Now what?"

"The nurse – she won't give me one – says they've got none to spare."

"It's okay, John," soothed Dr. Field. "You feel very warm and comfortable. Just like you had a large quilt over you."

Immediately I felt warmer. Then, I seemed to blank out.

After a couple of minutes Dr. Field asked me what was happening.

"Nothing. I'm nowhere."

After another moment or so my body started moving slowly back and forth. I began to feel very queasy – as if I were going to throw up. I could smell the ocean and feel the cold icy wind against my face. Then my eyes focused on the choppy, white-capped sea.

"Where are you now, John?"

"Aboard ship. It's very rough. And I'm seasick."

I groaned, then felt as though I were actually vomiting. Dr. Field intervened, suggesting to me that the seasickness would quickly go away. The sensation of upchucking soon passed, but I still felt cold and my chest ached from the damp.

"Where are you traveling to?"

"I'm headed home. This damned channel is always so choppy."

"The English Channel?"

"Yes. I'm on a troop ship with a bunch of the other casualties. Hope we don't run into a U-Boat before we get to Southampton."

"You're smiling."

"I was just thinking of my Maggie. She should be at the pier to meet the boat. I wrote her when I was coming. She probably won't recognize me – I'm so gaunt. But she'll have plenty of time to fatten me up now. I'm being discharged."

"How long has it been since you've seen Maggie?"

"Almost two years."

"What year is it?"

"1917. The war should be over pretty quick now that the Yanks have come in."

I began to feel very cold again. Dr. Field asked me why I was gripping my chest and scowling. I told her it was the chill sea wind. I was outside on deck, searching the far gray horizon. She asked me why I didn't get inside out of the cold.

"I want to see home – the English coastline." Suddenly it came into view. I got very excited. "There it is!" I cried out. I wanted to get out and push the ship to shore.

At last we were coming into port. The ship pulled up to the pier. There was a large crowd gathered, cheering us all and welcoming us back home. As I elbowed my way toward the gangplank, I eagerly tried to catch a glimpse of Maggie, but without success. My anxiety increased as I had to wait my turn to debark, because they were taking off so many of the wounded on stretchers.

Finally I was down on the pier. People were greeting eachother, crying and hugging – it was a very emotional scene. I searched and searched everywhere, but no Maggie. I began to feel panicky.

"Where the bloody hell is she?" I cried out as I raced up and down the dock, bumping into people and looking frantically in all directions. Dr. Field could see how agitated I was, so she gave me a suggestion to calm down. After a few moments I settled back. Then she asked, "What's happening now, John?"

"It's later. The crowd's thinning out. Still no sign of Maggie... Wait!"

"What is it?"

"There's an old lady dressed all in black – she's waving her brolly. She's coming toward me."

"Do you recognize her?"

"Yes. It's Maggie's mum. She looks so dismal. But then, she always did."

Old Mrs. Clive threw her arms around me, then gave me the terrible news. Maggie was gone – she'd run off with another man. Mrs. Clive couldn't have shocked me more if she'd punched me square in the face. At first I thought it was some ugly joke, but I quickly realized it was true.

"NO, damn it – NO!" I screamed. I went from fury to bitter disappointment in seconds. I started to sob.

"What is it, John?" Dr. Field asked.

"Maggie's gone!" I think I'd suspected something like that for some time, not having received any communication from her in months. But naturally I didn't want to believe it. Maggie's mother tried to comfort me, but I was inconsolable. She called her daughter "a tramp" and told me I was well rid of her. I continued to sob for some time; then, as a light rain began to fall, everything faded away.

From the Therapist's Perspective

"...all my troubles and obstacles have strengthened me...
You may not realize it when it happens,
but a kick in the teeth may be the best thing
in the world for you."
—Walt Disney

With Shawn's relating that he had been doing some home-work on his own, we began the next session of our journey back into the past. I was delighted that between sessions he had had some further breakthroughs. Anticipating that we would be able to tie the "bits and pieces" of his homework together, we ventured forward. But this was not to be the program for the day. Instead, once into hypnosis, Shawn journeyed elsewhere.

To start, John Williams was back in the hospital, once more in pain — pain all through his chest — pain all through his body. He was cold and he suffered from chills. Subsequently, he was on a ship crossing the English Channel. John was returning home from "The War". He was not only in pain, He was chilled and nauseated with seasickness from the pitching of the ship in the choppy waters. Here I empathized with John both personally and professionally. To my mind came the free association of the one time I had taken that voyage; as a schoolteacher, I had escorted a group of junior high students through Europe. As we crossed the channel, my seasickness from the rolling vessel tied one more knot in the strand of chaos that the travel agency had mistakenly referred to as a "Hellenic Holiday".

As for John, he was on the dock looking for his Maggie. He was so agitated because he could not find her, I finally had to suggest a calming effect. Shawn was panic stricken as he relived that scene. He clutched his chest and reported he was about to go into heart fibrillation. I did all I could to bring him back. To my dismay, Shawn went into the most intense display of emotions I had ever seen from him — perhaps from anyone.

Shawn angrily banged on the leather hassock before his chair. The hassock turned over on its side as though it could sustain no more abuse. Shawn screamed and pounded away. He punched and kicked it again and again. Then his anger turned into sadness as he culminated this episode. For many moments, Shawn sobbed and sobbed. I had no idea of where he was or what had occurred. He finally uttered, "Rain!"

It was as though the sky had shed tears along with him! Not until Shawn was out of trance did he explain his intense and explosive anger and sadness. It was the awful news brought to John at the dock. The "Lady in Black", Maggie's mum, was the bearer of bad news. He had lost his love, the lady he had so yearned for. She was not willing to await his return. John's awful physical pain was now to be accompanied by excruciating mental pain and anguish.

The intensity of the emotions displayed in this session brings forth the difference between "age regression" and what is known as "revivification". In age regression, the patient brings to memory all the knowledge and understanding of his present adult self. He is mostly aware of his presence in the present and is "looking back" at what occurred in his past. In revivification, the patient *becomes* the person in the past, as he actually relives the situation. It is as though he were presently experiencing the events for the first time.

Shawn was in one of the most intense revivification scenes I had ever witnessed. I had employed hypnosis for over two decades. Indeed, I had watched many individuals dramatically let go of feelings from the past. But never had I witnessed or experienced such an explosive release of emotions by a patient. Even Sigmund Freud had once declared that such release of pent-up feelings is the essence of psychotherapy. Shawn's catharsis was extraordinarily beautiful and awesome in its intensity. My heart went out to the man who was in such pain.

IV

An Unheroic Death

IV

AN UNHEROIC DEATH

As 1994 arrived, I was on my way to becoming a real V.I.P. – (*Very Incoherent Person*). Questions about these other-life experiences with Dr. Field had my brain bouncing back and forth so much the inside of my head felt like a handball court. Was I getting at something profoundly important, or just wasting a lot of mental energy? Was going through this process helping me get rid of my fears or was it just muddying the waters? Was my life in any way being improved? One thing that was definitely not improving was my relationship with Susan. During those first days of the new year it became clear that she was putting more and more space between us. There were numerous negative signals – sudden illnesses, last minute changes of plans, her need to work extra long hours. While most of her reasons for putting me off seemed a bit thin, it was certainly true that she was having a tough time on the job. A new boss at her agency was putting a lot of pressure on her. She was especially ticked off at being moved out of her office by a another executive. Even so, Susan had been through this kind of thing before and I'd never known anyone more skilled at rolling with the punches. Apart from the difficulties of dealing with new management, something else was clearly bothering her. I knew that "something else" was me.

I'd recently gotten up the nerve to tell her I was going to therapy. We'd just finished dinner at her place and were both pretty relaxed, so I thought I'd chosen the right moment. She took the news surprisingly well, but when I attempted to sidestep her questions about why I was seeing a psychologist, she rightly grew impatient. I fumbled around with my bad weather problem, trying to make it seem not terribly serious and yet worth seeing a shrink about. This of course sounded pretty phoney and only succeeded in irritating Susan. She said that maybe if I'd had any "real" problems I wouldn't be so preoccupied with myself and wouldn't need to see a therapist – exactly the reaction I'd feared. It really made me mad, but what could I say? In trying to fudge the issue I'd only made matters worse. I wanted to lash out, but instead I swallowed my feelings, said goodnight and left.

As I drove off, I got angrier and angrier – not at Susan, but at myself. I'd really screwed things up badly. I should've honestly explained my terror of wind and rain. But then, how could I explain something I didn't understand? And if she was turned off by my being so preoccupied with myself, what would she have said about my delving into a previous existence? It's bad enough to be self-involved with one person, but self-involved with TWO persons?

When I got home, there was a message from Susan on my answering machine. She was very sorry for what she'd said to me. I called her back and we patched things up for the moment, but the air was still going out of our relationship. And yet, even though Susan was keeping me at arm's length, I still held out hope that I'd soon get past all this weirdness and we'd rediscover each other all over again. But still another detour in our journey to romance appeared a few days later. We'd taken a Caribbean cruise the year before. We'd had a marvelous time and wanted to do it again. We'd talked enthusiastically about another trip for months, but then she started backing off, saying she might not want to go after all. She used her work as a reason for her uncertainty. Things were growing more precarious and she didn't feel comfortable about taking the time off. At first I felt her job jitters were an overreaction and in time everything would fall into place. But the deadline for booking the trip was drawing near. I had to get a yes or a no from Susan. She gave me a no. She said I should go by myself. Ugh!

During my next appointment with Dr. Field we did no hypnotic work. We talked instead about how things were falling apart with Susan and me. Her decision to forego the cruise was a real blow. It only pointed up to me how far I'd fallen in her eyes. How could I blame her? A silly middle-aged man scared stiff of wind and rainstorms? Who could warm up to that?

Dr. Field, as usual, looked on the bright side. She thought there was a real possibility that Susan in time might get used to the idea that I had a genuine problem and even respect the fact that I was doing my best to solve it. When I expressed my doubts, Dr. Field suggested I bring Susan with me to one of our sessions. That idea appealed even less to me than I thought it might to Susan. It would've been like inviting her to my dermatologist's office so she could watch him lance a boil on my butt. I don't know which one of us would've been grossed out more. While I didn't use this particular metaphor with Dr. Field, I believe I got my message across.

Later on, we reviewed what had recently come out of my past-life regressions, trying to put them in some kind of perspective. Apart from the connection of a horrible war experience which included terrible weather, I saw no link with the events of my "real" life. But then Dr. Field brought up a painful possibility about Maggie, my John Williams run-away wife.

"Do you think there might be a parallel between Susan and Maggie?" she asked.

At first I had a kind of knee-jerk denial reaction. "I don't see it. Susan is one classy lady. Maggie's own mother called her a tramp. Susan could never be put in that category."

"I'm not suggesting that."

"Then what do you mean?"

"Only that Maggie left you and now you're afraid Susan's going to do the same thing."

A real wave of terror suddenly went through me. Something ominous was stirring just beneath the surface of my awareness. I would soon confront this monster from my ocean floor – the beast I dreaded more than anything – my fear of abandonment.

Throughout my adult life I'd had a number of relationships with women, but none had ever led to a lasting commitment. I'd never made a conscious decision to stay single, yet the question now arose. Had I kept myself from walking into marriage because I so dreaded the anguish of being walked out on? But if this were true, where did this fear come from? There had been no breakup in my life as Shawn Regan that even came close to producing the agony I suffered when Maggie abandoned John Williams. It was hard to believe that my beast from below could have grown so terrifying from the much less intense rejections in Shawn Regan's life. It seemed like it had to have been nurtured somewhere else. For the first time, I began to lean toward the possibility that I really had lived before.

At the conclusion of our session, Dr. Field once again encouraged me to use some self-hypnosis to see what other "facts" from the life of John Williams I could retrieve. The next day, January 7, was a significant date in this regard. I'd slept late, having swam many lengths of the pool at my gym the night before to work off my frustration at once more being put off by Susan. I awoke feeling very loose and refreshed. As I lay half awake in bed, I gave myself the suggestion that I was going to go into an altered state of consciousness. Because I was already so relaxed, it didn't take long to drift back to the life and times of John Williams. More bits of information started to dance across my mental scanner.

Some of the same situations I'd experienced earlier came up before my mind's eye, but this time in greater detail. I was again on a ship crossing the channel, once more feeling the pitch and roll of the waves and the queasy feeling in my stomach. I looked up and down the length of the large ship and I was the only one on deck. The weather was terrible, and the salt spray from the windblown waves was stinging my face, but I was so anxious to see England come up over the horizon I was getting soaked. Then I felt someone grab me by the shoulder and turn me around. It was a sailor. He was furious at me and told me to get below before I got swept overboard.

Time then seemed to go ahead a few years. It was the early nineteen twenties. As I had experienced the previous time I'd done this exercise, I was in my London shoe shop. This time I was arranging a window display of the latest in men's footwear. It seemed as though business was good. I then locked the door and went up the street. It was mid-day and there were many people walking about. The street was packed with vintage automobiles and taxis. The smell of coal dust mixed with auto exhaust filled the air. As I walked briskly along, I could see my reflection in the store windows. I stopped for a moment, pretending to look at the merchandise inside one of the shops, but I was actually admiring my reflection. I was very nattily attired in a tailored brown suit and a bowler hat. I'd put back on the weight I'd lost during the war. My mustache was neatly trimmed down.

Next I walked into a pub – the same pub I'd been in previously. It was very smokey inside. Through the haze I could see a row of glasses hanging over the bar. I said hello to some people who were sitting at tables. Apparently we were all "regulars". They returned my greeting. A woman appeared behind the bar. It was Molly, the same one I'd seen before. She smiled and greeted me warmly. She seemed to know exactly what I wanted. She took one of the glasses down from the overhead rack and poured me a drink. This seemed like my usual routine. Molly asked me if I wanted anything to eat. I said, "No." I couldn't wait to down my drink.

Time went forward again. It was years later – the early thirties. Now I was walking on a train platform. The sky was grey and I was very despondent. I felt woozy, as if sick or drunk. I couldn't seem to get my bearings. I put my hand out to lean against a post but lost my balance. Then I fell off the platform onto the tracks below.

I almost flew out of bed at this point, shocked back to full wakefulness. My heart was pounding through my chest. It was an awful experience, very much like getting stabbed with the bayonet. I had to wonder if this was the way John Williams died. I sprang out of bed, turned on the radio really loud and dressed quickly, trying to put this very disturbing denouement to my experiment in auto-regression out of my head.

That weekend was perfect for letting go of troubling thoughts. It included a wedding and a birthday party. Susan was more upbeat than I'd seen her for a long time, crying buckets of joyful tears when the minister pronounced the bride and groom man and wife. At both the reception and at the birthday bash she was in her glory, socializing with her wide circle of friends and acquaintances. I didn't know many of the people at these functions, but it made me feel really good to see Susan so happy. The party atmosphere was just what the doctor ordered for both of us, taking her mind off her work problems and distracting me from my constant John Williams befuddlement.

Sunday morning Susan and I slept in, made love and then had a big late breakfast. We'd enjoyed one of the best weekends ever, that is, right up to the end. Unfortunately, it finished on a familiar but sour note – my being in therapy. I don't know how the subject came up. I'd tried my damndest for two days to avoid it, but here it was again. Susan still didn't understand why I couldn't just deal with my problem myself. I tried to explain that there were loads of problems I could solve alone – everything from writing a cartoon story to fixing a flat tire to working a Rubic's Cube. But trying to unravel this knotted ball of mental twine was more than I could handle on my own. She shook her head, threw up her hands and said, "Well, you do what you have to do." I said, "Fine. That's what I'll do." We left it at that. I went home feeling pretty bad about myself and about our relationship.

Monday began with a real test. A strong Santana wind came up, blowing hard most of the day. Surprisingly, even though it still gave me the jitters, I was able to get a day's work in, despite the spooky horror movie sounds that always accompany these winds. I even took a long walk while the blustery breezes were kicking up. I felt a victory of sorts, the kind only someone with this strange type of hangup could appreciate. Again, I wondered if my tiny triumph over the elements had anything to do with my therapy or with the regressions. I couldn't see the connection, but maybe Dr. Field could.

I brought up my minor success when we got together the next day. She was quick to praise me and told me not to discount my newfound "strength". It might seem trivial to most people, but for me it was like a man with a broken leg getting his cast off and taking his first steps. As far as a tie-in between this and my past-life journeys, she felt there probably was a link, but the precise nature of it still wasn't clear.

We then discussed my weekend with Susan and how it had ended so badly. I felt this was one more big wedge between Susan and me and I feared she was getting ready to part company. Dr. Field urged me not to give up hope, that I was starting to make real progress. The new way I'd dealt with the fearful wind had indicated as much. Susan might soon see that what I was doing was working.

Toward the end of the hour I related to Dr. Field my most recent experiment in auto-regression. Although I didn't spell out every detail, I emphasized how much more vivid it had all been this time. She was quite excited about this whole past-life picture, so much so that she proposed that we video tape our next hypnotic session. The idea immediately threw me. I'm not especially shy, but the notion of seeing myself as someone else was off-putting, to say the least. At first I refused to do it. But Dr. Field could be very persuasive. She finally won me over by convincing me that this might well be a really important step in my therapeutic process. Reluctantly, I agreed.

From the Therapist's Perspective

*"One thing is sure, there are just two respectable ways to die.
One is of old age, and the other is by accident."*
—Gilbert Hubbard, *The Philistine*

And so it was 1994. The year of the BIG BLAST here in Los Angeles. And more of a blast for Shawn as well.

His relationship with Susan seemed on the rocks. In a way it was beginning to mirror the John and Maggie finale. But I had hoped Shawn would give it all he could before he gave up. I knew how much he wanted it to work. A break-up with Susan would certainly not help Shawn's fragile persona at this time. We psychologists do our best to encourage anything but major life changes when other issues are at hand.

Susan was definitely not one to applaud psychotherapy. Psychologists believe that it is the healthy person that enters into therapy. People usually seek help when they become aware that they need to work with a skilled mental health professional. Eventually, with the guidance of the therapist, they will discover their own inner resources, their Wizard Within, which will take them along the journey to a positive and healthy resolution.

Shawn would have adored Susan for supporting his situation and working to fix it. But that was not to be. Support from Susan, the Significant Other, was not happening. Even so, I encouraged him to give it his all. Maybe when she saw some improvement — which was already in its beginning phases — just maybe she would bend.

Often, bringing the partner into the therapy can help this person to understand, and that can make a big difference. But even Shawn was not for that. I guess he foresaw Susan's reaction on that one.

I couldn't help thinking about the beautiful trip to the Caribbean and how many other ladies would have enjoyed accompanying this handsome and pleasant man to those islands with their delightful beaches, the exciting Calypso music, and the historic sites. Yet, Shawn was destined to go single.

The parallel between this situation and that with Maggie did not jive with Shawn. But when I suggested the abandonment issue, all hell broke loose. For sure, something really clicked. Shawn looked like I'd hit him over the head, and just maybe I had. Why had he remained single all his life? A fear of being abandoned was apparent throughout his therapy. But why? Nothing we'd talked about in the sessions supported his having ever been deserted in this life. Oh, yes, his mother had left him in his baby carriage one day while she was shopping. Little Shawny had tried to climb out to see where she went and tipped over the carriage with its many grocery items. This, of course, did anything but delight Mama who punished him for his ungainly egress. There were numerous other instances of early childhood mischief which incurred the wrath of his mother, such as writing on a window with a stick of butter, or drawing on the walls with his crayons, or following his older brother and sister to school. These and many other forgotten scenarios emerged in our hypnotic sessions. However, I really doubt that such relatively minor issues could be responsible for his overwhelming feelings of abandonment. So where did these feelings come from?

He'd told me more than once that if he married or had a permanent relationship, he had a strong fear that the woman would leave him. Was this just an excuse not to march to the altar or did this phobia come from a real traumatic event?

Subsequent to this meeting, at my suggestion, Shawn did some more homework. This brought forth another incident with John Williams and Molly, the barmaid in a "Cheers" scene from out of the past. Molly's asking John if he would have something to eat was not a question she asked all of her patrons. We would learn in later sessions just how special John was to her.

As that rather pleasant occurrence took a back seat, Shawn, as John, then found himself on a train platform. Woozy and disoriented, and possibly drunk, he lost his balance and fell to the tracks below. This very upsetting incident was also to come up again later and take on a significant meaning. Meanwhile, Shawn's terrified reaction to it suggested its relevance.

As for the moment, Shawn stood the test of a really bad blast from a strong Santana wind. For the first time since he started therapy, he was able to function despite its fury. And, I must admit, the sounds of that Santana were very scary. But Shawn got through it. He did his work and even went for a wonderful walk in the wind. I couldn't praise him enough for this heroic achievement. Indeed, one needs to be the victim of this kind of phobia to appreciate the meaning of such a victory.

V

On
The Train

V

ON THE TRAIN
January 12, 1994 Video Taped Session

*T*he following is a verbatim transcript, taken from the video tape. As I mentioned in the previous chapter, I was full of apprehension as I entered this session. I suppose a good deal of it was simply stage fright. I also worried that, in being too self-conscious, I might fail to go into trance and wind up with egg on my face. However, thanks to Dr. Field's skill, that was not a problem. I was able to relax, allowing myself to bring up a great deal of valuable information from my "former self".

Dr. Field put me into a trance state using one of her methods. In a few minutes I was in a fairly deep trance.

DR. F: "Now I'd like you to just concentrate on yourself today. The fact that we do have a video on is removed from your mind. The word I just mentioned, you are no longer to think about. It isn't here. You feel comfortable. You feel relaxed. It doesn't matter what really happens because our only interest is you. And what we learn today. Just let yourself relax as much as you can. Let yourself go deeper and further. Deeper. That's right. With each and every breath you take, you go into a deeper and more relaxed state. You're going deeper and deeper – as though you're going down in an elevator, escalator or stairway. As you go down, with each step, with each floor – deeper and deeper. Today we plan to go back to the past, to some of those episodes to which we've been before. It seems that as I was stroking your chest on the initial time we did this; this caused you to go back."

Dr. Field rises from her chair and touches my upper chest.

DR. F: "That's why I'm here now, doing the same thing. Making you so comfortable, but at the same time, letting you carry yourself back in time."

Dr. Field strokes my forehead.

DR. F: "Back as though you were on a very special train – with a very special chord by your seat, which you can pull at any time to make it stop or make it start. Because you are in control."

I start to grimace and twist my head back and forth.

DR. F: "That's right, Shawn. Just stay with it. (Whispers) Take you back… back…"

I continue to frown and twitch as she continues:

DR. F: "Faster and faster, it's going back in time, until you arrive at a point in time, somewhere…let a "yes" finger lift when you arrive."

My index finger rises.

DR. F: "I see a finger showing me to validate… Good."

Dr. Field resumes her seat. I begin to turn from side to side with a pained look.

DR. F: "Stay with what's happening. Experience for yourself what's going on."

I start to groan.

SHAWN: "Ooh! Ooh! Ooh!"

Dr. Field touches my hand.

DR. F: "Focus in on the feeling."

I continue to roll my head and moan.

DR. F: "At any time you care to talk, you may do so, or just simply share it with yourself."

I rub my upper chest with my right hand.

DR. F: "Start with that feeling. Focus in on the feeling. Forget the thoughts in your head and stay with those physical sensations."

I begin to cough.

SHAWN: "It hurts."

DR. F: "Your chest hurts?"

I nod yes.

SHAWN: "I was riding on the train."

DR. F: "On the train?"

SHAWN: "Yes. Moving around hurts. It's the old wound."

DR. F: "The old wound?"

SHAWN: "Wish I had one of my pills. Ooh, moving around on the train – it doesn't help."

DR. F: "Where are you going on the train?"

SHAWN: "The country. I'm going to the south of England. To Brighton."

DR. F: "To Brighton in the south of England?"

I nod yes. All this time I have been rubbing my upper chest with my right hand.

SHAWN: "For a vacation."

DR. F: "Where do you live?"

SHAWN: "In London."

DR. F: "What year is this?"

SHAWN: "This is 1920. The wound still hurts."

I continue to grimace and rub my chest.

DR. F: "The wound is still acting up?"

SHAWN: "It never stops. And it's considerably damp today. It's been hurting."

DR. F: "How long has it been since you were wounded?"

SHAWN: "Oh, God – three, four years, I guess. I'm just going down for a holiday."

DR. F: "Is the war over?"

SHAWN: "Yeah, yeah. I'm going down there. It's a little warmer there. Going to get a little sun."

DR. F: "Are you going alone?"

SHAWN: "Yeah."

DR. F: "Where's your wife?"

SHAWN: "Oh, no, no. Don't talk about her."

DR. F: "You don't want to talk about her?"

SHAWN: "I want to have some fun. I don't want to talk about her."

DR. F: "I understand. You want to have some fun. You don't want to talk about her."

SHAWN: "It's better now."

DR. F: "Feeling better now."

SHAWN: "I go over some rough places there. And it hurts, you know."

I breathe deeply.

DR. F: "How old are you?"

SHAWN: "Twenty-four."

DR. F: "Twenty-four now."

SHAWN: "I feel like I'm about a hundred and four. This thing, you know."

I rub my chest.

SHAWN: "It's, it's – this cold, you know. In cold weather it just gets me."

DR. F: "Would you like to take that feeling back to where it started from? The origin of that?"

SHAWN: "Oh, I know where it came from. I don't want to do that again."

DR. F: "Don't want to go back?"

SHAWN: "No, no. Ugh!"

DR. F: "Shall we travel forward to Brighton?"

SHAWN: "Yeah. Let's do."

DR. F: "Good."

I lean back and breathe deeply.

DR. F: "The train is going forward now. See yourself on the train – "

As Dr. Field speaks, I continue to breathe heavily.

" – There's a comfortable white linen napkin beneath your head."

SHAWN: "Yeah."

DR. F: "Can you feel the comfort of that?"

SHAWN: "Nice."

DR. F: "What do you see out the window?"

SHAWN: "Oh, it's just the country going by – it's kind of pretty today. Just wish it could be a little warmer."

I continue to rub my chest with my right hand.

DR. F: "No sun today?"

SHAWN: "No, but it'll get better."

DR. F: "Can you see the green of the countryside?"

SHAWN: "Oh, yeah. It's been so damp and foggy. I've had enough of that."

DR. F: "Dampness and wet and fog. Don't want to talk about that either?"

SHAWN: "Well, you know, it's England."

DR. F: "Yeah – How long have you lived in England?"

SHAWN: "Oh, since I was a kid."

I make a gesture with my hand, as if showing how little I was.

SHAWN: "Used to live up in the north country."

DR. F: "North country? What was the name of your home town – or the province – "

SHAWN: "Oh, it was up in Lancashire. What was the name of the place...?"

I turn my head, as if trying to recall.

"... A wee town. A little place."

Again the hand gesture indicating how small it was.

DR. F: "Did you live there with your mother and your father?"

SHAWN: "Yeah. Both of them."

DR. F: "What made them move? Or did you move?"

SHAWN: "I moved away. I moved down aways when I decided to get a trade. And I got an apprenticeship."

DR. F: "Doing what?"

SHAWN: "Bootmaking. In Kent. Or it's further south than that..."

I rub my forehead as I try to recall.

SHAWN: "...I get confused. I can't remember where anything is."

DR. F: "You're confused at the geography of England?"

SHAWN: "Yeah. It's uh, it seems like I've been away a long time."

DR. F: "Have you been away a long time?"

SHAWN: "It's like I'm revisiting everything."

DR. F: "Like you're revisiting?"

SHAWN: "Yes. It's like I've gone back home after a long visit someplace."

DR. F: "Where have you been?"

I shake my head as if baffled.

SHAWN: "Someplace else."

DR. F: "Do you like bootmaking and shoemaking?"

SHAWN: "I used to. Used to like it a lot. But lately, I don't know."

DR. F: "You need another challenge?"

SHAWN: "Yeah. I just got restless, you know. This going away now, just got to get out of the city and shake the cobwebs out a little..."

I rub my chest.

SHAWN: "... and try to get a little relief from this."

DR. F: "Think the warmth will make it feel better?"

SHAWN: "Sure."

DR. F: "You want to tell me where that (pain in the chest) came from?"

SHAWN: "The wound? Oh, it was in the war. The big war."

DR. F: "What did they call that war?"

SHAWN: "The World War. I was in France. That bugger. He stuck me good."

I continue to rub my chest.

DR. F: "Who 'stuck you good'?"

SHAWN: "That bloody Kraut."

DR. F: "That 'bloody Kraut' stuck you good?"

SHAWN: "Yeah. They got him though, I understand, later. I went out, you know. I just – I thought I was gone. But they got him."

DR. F: "They did get him, huh?"

SHAWN: "They got him."

DR. F: "They say what comes around goes around."

SHAWN: "Well they got him. He was just, you know, he just come running like a fool, you know. He, he wasn't even with the rest of his bunch there, you know. He just came running on his own and come flying into the trench with the bayonet stuck out and I just happened to be in the wrong place, you know. He cut me right here."

I point to my upper chest.

SHAWN: "They got him right away though. He was a fool. It was ridiculous to do that."

DR. F: "He cut you there. Did you end up in the hospital?"

SHAWN: "Oh, yeah. Oh, Jesus."

DR. F: (Laughs) "Oh Jesus? How long were you in the hospital?"

SHAWN: "Oh, shit – forever! Excuse my language."

DR. F: "That's fine. I use that language too. You were in the hospital forever?"

SHAWN: "Ah, it was... tubes and things stuck in me... stitches and bandages and all that stuff, you know. God!"

I gesture several times, pointing toward my neck and upper body.

SHAWN: "You wouldn't think that just a little stick in the chest would do that to you, but, I guess I'm lucky to be alive."

DR. F: "You are lucky to be alive. I guess it's a time you don't like to look back to."

SHAWN: "No. No."

DR. F: "A stressful time?"

SHAWN: "Not as difficult as – we had the flu."

DR. F: "You had the flu?"

SHAWN: "You know the flu epidemic killed so many people."

DR. F: "The flu killed so many people? Was that after you came back?"

SHAWN: "Yeah. It was all over the world after the war was over. All the lads came home and brought the bugs with them. So many people died."

DR. F: "I didn't know that. The lads came home and brought the bugs with them? Did you get the flu too?"

SHAWN: "No."

DR. F: "You didn't. You had your share already."

SHAWN: "Yeah."

I grimace and again rub my chest.

SHAWN: "Uh! I'm getting cold again. I'm sorry. I've got to put a wrap on. It's this damn thing, you know."

Dr. Field rises from her chair and gestures as though she is putting a blanket around my shoulders.

DR. F: "Is that going to do it?"

SHAWN: "Yeah, that's real cozy. Thanks."

DR. F: "Nice sitting with you on the train and talking about experiences."

SHAWN: "It's a pleasure."

DR. F: "You're feeling better now?"

SHAWN: "Yeah."

DR. F: "Anything else happen back there that was kind of upsetting to you? Must be hard going through a war… coming home again."

SHAWN: "Oh, you know, all the lads had to face it."

DR. F: "I guess we women are lucky. We don't go to war."

SHAWN: "It wasn't easy on anybody."

DR. F: "No. Hope there'll never be another war."

SHAWN: "Oh, God, no! I guess they're having a problem in Ireland."

DR. F: "What's happening in Ireland? I haven't been keeping up with – "

SHAWN: "Oh, the 'trouble', you know – the damned I.R.A.. You know I've got relatives in Ireland. I come from there, really. At least my family."

DR. F: "Your family comes from there? What's your last name?"

SHAWN: "Williams."

DR. F: "Williams?"

SHAWN: "Yeah. The old man was born in Ireland. My mother in England, but we're really kind of half and half here."

DR. F: "You're half Irish."

SHAWN: "Yeah. Well, you can see it on my face."

DR. F: "Yeah, yeah. You look Irish. Those freckles. What's happening in Ireland now?"

SHAWN: "Oh, they're just blowing up everything."

DR. F: "I guess this world will never be at peace."

SHAWN: "It's the same up in the north country."

DR. F: "What's happening up in the north country?"

SHAWN: "It's the same old thing – the Catholics and the Church of England. At least the Irish got their freedom – they're an independent state now."

DR. F: "Where are your relatives? Are they in the north country now?"

SHAWN: "Well, I don't know anymore. It's been a long time. There are some cousins and people – oh, they're spread all over the place – Limerick, Kerry, all over. I don't have any contact with them."

DR. F: "Any of you come from Dublin?"

SHAWN: "There are some there too."

DR. F: "Where are you from?

SHAWN: "I was born in Lancashire."

DR. F: "Just the family came from Ireland?"

SHAWN: "Just my father. He was born in... Kerry, I think.... Kilkerry?"

DR. F: "I've never been there. Is it pretty country?"

SHAWN: "Cold and wet!"

DR. F: "Colder and wetter than England?"

SHAWN: "I don't think it could be any colder and wetter than it is here. But it's just as cold and just as wet there."

DR. F: "In the war – where did you fight?"

SHAWN: "In France. Belgium and France.... Sarajevo? .... Where is that?"

I look off, as if searching my memory. (Note: World War I started in Sarajevo, which is in Bosnia.)

DR. F: "I guess my geography is not too good. You'll have to tell me."

SHAWN: "I was in Ypres (pronounced, 'Eep')."

DR. F: "Where?"

SHAWN: "Ypres. Eepers! You know it?"

DR. F: "Eepers? And that's in France?"

SHAWN: "We used to call it, 'Eepers-Jeepers'. It's Y-P-R-E-S or some dumb thing. We called it, 'EEP'."

DR. F: "That's in France?"

SHAWN: "That's in France…"

(Note: It's actually in Belgium.)

SHAWN: "… We were all over. We had this terrible rain and rain and rain and mud. Digging holes. Digging and marching and digging."

DR. F: "Marching and digging. And it would rain?"

SHAWN: "Ugh! All the time. Mud."

DR. F: "Wind too?"

SHAWN: "Wind and mud and rain. Oh geez! I wondered would I ever get warm! Ever since then, having this – "

I touch my chest again.

SHAWN: " – and that – these two things – I think one of these days I'm going to have to take me out of this country and go somewhere where it's warm. I'm only twenty-four years old and I can't take it. Imagine what it's going to be like when I'm up in years."

DR. F: "You really need to get out of this country and go where it's warm."

SHAWN: "I do, yeah."

DR. F: "Where is it warm around here?"

SHAWN: "Brighton, you know – It's a nice place. It's warmer down there."

DR. F: "Well, this is my first trip down here – "

SHAWN: "We've even got palm trees here."

DR. F: "Palm trees in Brighton?"

SHAWN: "Yeah…"

I point.

SHAWN: " …Look out there. There they are. See them?"

DR. F: "Oh. We're approaching the city?"

SHAWN: "Right there. We're coming in. Yeah. It's kind of grey out though. Of course, it's early – it's early in the year. And you can't expect it to be too warm this time of the year anyway. But I just had to get out of the city."

DR. F: "I think you did yourself a nice favor to get away from the city and come down here. How many miles are we training down here from the – "

SHAWN: " – Oh, it's about ninety miles. It's not that long by train. Only a couple of hours."

DR. F: "Are we almost there?"

SHAWN: "Yeah, we're pulling in now. Have you been here before?"

DR. F: "I've not been here. This is my first trip down here."

SHAWN: "Well, I've been here before. But it's funny. It's so..."

I make a gesture by my head, denoting some confusion.

SHAWN: " ...I feel like I've been away a long time."

DR. F: "You feel like you've been away a long time?"

SHAWN: "Yeah."

I start to shiver.

SHAWN: "I hate to shiver in front of you, but I feel so – I have this problem, you know..."

I wrap my arms around my torso.

SHAWN: "... Sometimes I just get the shakes."

DR. F: "That's okay. You do what you need to do. Don't worry about me. I'm just here."

SHAWN: "I just can't... I'm a little ashamed to shake in front of a nice lady, but I just – "

DR. F: "It's okay to shake in front of anybody. You're feeling the shakes. How long have you had shakes? Since the war?"

SHAWN: "Well, it's the cold here."

DR. F: "Even with that blanket?"

I rub my face.

SHAWN: "Well, I think it's...you know, just between you and me, I think I have a little bit of nerves too from the war."

DR. F: "A bit of nerves?"

SHAWN: "From all the bomb blasts. It gets to you."

DR. F: "The bomb blasts?"

SHAWN: "Yeah. It shakes you up. You never get a night's sleep. And you go long enough without sleep and, I don't know, you get the shakes. You wake up at night sometimes with the shakes."

DR. F: "You wake up with the shakes. You still get the shakes, even with the war over?"

SHAWN: "Now I got them, but only because of the..."

DR. F: "The cold?"

SHAWN: "...I guess it just hurts me sometimes."

DR. F: "In your chest? Does it feel like – "

SHAWN: "It's just the shakes."

DR. F: "Pretty soon we'll be in Brighton and you'll be okay."

SHAWN: "You know, some people think I hit the sauce a little too hard!" (I laugh.)

DR. F: "Do you hit the sauce a little too hard?"

SHAWN: "Well, I suppose I do."

DR. F: (She laughs.)

SHAWN: "But it warms you up, you know. It gives you a little bit of a glow. Sometimes too much. You know I've been bartending."

DR. F: "You've been bartending?"

SHAWN: "Yeah."

DR. F: "Is that what you've been doing? In addition to making shoes?"

SHAWN: "I've been kind of shirking my work lately. I shouldn't but I've been closing up earlier and earlier."

DR. F: "What club do you work in?"

SHAWN: "To the... the dog... What's the dog...?"

I point to my nose.

SHAWN: "The pup or something... the dog, the wild dog, or the mad dog... some kind of a dog. Red Dog. I think it's the Red Dog."

DR. F: "I think I've heard of it. Bet you serve a lot of beer there."

SHAWN: "Lot of beer. Lot of Guinness. Lot of ale. Al, you know, he runs the place. He's seen me in there so often, he says, 'You're in here so often why don't you work here?'"

DR. F: "So is that how you got the bartending job?"

SHAWN: "We've got to close down for awhile at tea time."

DR. F: "Close down?"

SHAWN: "We've got to do that – it's a new dumb law. We have to close at four and open up again after supper. I think that was because too many of the lads coming back and drinking too much. That's why they put that law in."

DR. F: "Too many brawls in the pub perhaps, huh?"

SHAWN: "Oh, just too much drinking."

DR. F: "Too much drinking. Good Irish whiskey there?"

SHAWN: "Oh, yes."

DR. F: "I like that in my coffee sometime. Some whipped cream on top."

SHAWN: "It's not just the drinking. It's the economy. The depression."

DR. F: "You look calmer now. Did the shakes go away?"

SHAWN: "I'm still a little cold. But I'll be okay soon."

DR. F: "You never told me your full name."

SHAWN: "It's Johnny."

DR. F: "May I call you Johnny?"

SHAWN: "Sure. That's what everybody calls me. Johnny. Johnny H. For John Henry."

DR. F: "And I'm Sandy. You can call me Sandy."

SHAWN: "Sandy. Nice to meet you, Sandy."

DR. F: "Nice to meet you, Johnny."

SHAWN: "I guess we'll be getting off the train soon."

DR. F: "I guess I'll be gone. I've never been here before. I'm visiting some friends down here."

SHAWN: "You'll love it. It's got the nice beach and all."

DR. F: "Just what I need. Everybody loves the beach."

SHAWN: "Get some sun. I'm sure we'll get some sun before long."

DR. F: "Okay, John. Can we move forward to your vacation?"

SHAWN: "Yeah."

Dr. Field rises from her chair and makes a few passes with her hand over my face and head. She then resumes her seat.

DR. F: "Where are you?"

SHAWN: "In my room."

DR. F: "It's a hotel?"

SHAWN: "Yes. It's a hotel. It's a nice place. It's a small place. It's kind of off-season so there's not too many people here. But I have my feet up and I'm looking out the window here. Very nice."

DR. F: "Is it warm?"

SHAWN: "Well, it could be warmer."

DR. F: "Are you going to go swimming in that ocean?"

SHAWN: "Oh, God, no!" (I laugh).

DR. F: "That would be too cold. Did you ever go swimming in cold water before?"

SHAWN: "Oh, sure – but it never gets warm here – the water."

DR. F: "Do you go outdoors? Experience some of the warm sunshine?"

SHAWN: "Well, I will, yes. I'll go take a walk later. It's just a little nippy out there."

DR. F: "Does it ever rain down here?"

SHAWN: "Oh, sure. But it's always a little warmer here."

DR. F: "A nice ocean breeze?"

SHAWN: "Well it's the current. What do they call that current? It's the current. It comes along here and keeps things warm."

I start to rub my face and hunch my shoulders, as if in some distress.

DR. F: "You like the ocean breeze now?"

SHAWN: "I've always loved the ocean. I do indeed."

DR. F: "What are you feeling? Are you in a nice place?"

SHAWN: "Well, you know, I'm not sure I should've come."

DR. F: "You're not sure you should've come?"

SHAWN: "Well, you know, it brings back memories."

DR. F: "Memories of what?"

SHAWN: (I whisper) "Maggie and me."

DR. F: "Who is Maggie?"

SHAWN: "Maggie's my wife."

DR. F: "What happened to Maggie?"

SHAWN: "Well, she just took off. She couldn't take the waiting."

DR. F: "Couldn't take the waiting?"

SHAWN: "No. She just... She was just too busy to... You know, she couldn't sit still, I guess, or something, I don't know."

DR. F: "She couldn't sit still? Which – "

SHAWN: " – Well, when I was over in the war, you know. We got married just a short time before I went."

DR. F: "It's hard when you get married just before you leave for war."

SHAWN: "Yeah, we shouldn't have done it, I suppose, but everybody was – you never knew if you were going to come back."

DR. F: "Then what happened?"

SHAWN: "Well, she just up and left me."

DR. F: "Did she write you a letter?"

SHAWN: "No. No, no. Her old mom told me."

DR. F: "Where'd you see her mom?"

SHAWN: "She met me at the ship."

DR. F: "Well, that was nice of her mom to do that."

SHAWN: "Yes it was. She's a great old gal."

DR. F: "That must've been very upsetting. What did you feel when she – "

SHAWN: "Well, I'm kind of over it now, but – "

DR. F: "Good. You're over it now."

SHAWN: "Well, I guess I still love her. Well, the old man was a Catholic and we really never went to church much, but, I don't know, I've still got this thing about getting married. I just don't... You know we never really got divorced."

DR. F: "You're not divorced and your father was a Catholic. Does that mean you don't get married again?"

SHAWN: "Well, I don't know, because I'm not that religious, you know. I just have a feeling about it, that once you're married, then that's it."

DR. F: "Of course, if she's gone, then we've got to let go somewhere, don't we?"

SHAWN: "I suppose."

DR. F: "I bet it's because you're really feeling something still inside you, aren't you?"

I don't answer – I just shake my head and frown.

DR. F: "Would it be alright, SHAWN, to get in touch with those feelings?"

I don't respond.

DR. F: "Johnny?"

This gets my attention.

SHAWN: "What?"

DR. F: "Would it be alright to get in touch with those feelings?"

SHAWN: "What? You mean with Maggie?"

DR. F: "Yeah."

I frown and turn away.

SHAWN: "Oh, do we have to rake over that old... ugh!"

DR. F: "It might be a good idea to do it just because you don't want to – it might be good to do it."

SHAWN: "Well, if you must."

DR. F: "Well, why don't you just forget the thoughts in your head while you're in this nice wonderful place in Brighton."

I look off.

SHAWN: "It looks like the sun's coming out."

DR. F: "Good."

SHAWN: "It's just going down. It's funny. It's the end of the day and it's the first time we're seeing the sun. Well, maybe tomorrow."

I continue to look off to my right.

DR. F: "It' so nice when the sun has gone down and you're in a beautiful place. Just put your hand where you're feeling it the most and just let yourself drift back to Maggie and what you're really feeling."

I don't respond. I sit glumly with my arms folded.

DR. F: "You go back for a moment, back, back, back, to when you arrived back and her mother was waiting for you."

Again, I don't respond.

DR. F: "Let yourself get in touch with the sensation – that feeling – FEEL the feeling."

I groan and shake my head. Then a long pause before I respond.

SHAWN: "The first thing I do is I get mad at Maggie's mom."

DR. F: "What do you tell her when you get mad at her?"

SHAWN: "Oh, I don't want to repeat that. I called her some bad names."

DR. F: "Well, you were upset. People use bad names as a way of getting it out."

SHAWN: "I didn't believe her. I didn't want to believe her at first. I thought she was just there to... I don't know what I thought. I just couldn't believe what she was telling me."

DR. F: "You didn't believe it."

SHAWN: "But then I realized... I kind of feared it anyway."

DR. F: "You feared it ahead of time?"

SHAWN: "Yeah. She didn't write. She stopped writing to me. But then I thought maybe they're just not getting me her letters because we're out there where they can't get the mail, you know, and maybe she had written me. I didn't know. I just had the fear, you know, I just didn't want to believe it."

DR. F: "But you had the fear."

I begin rubbing my stomach.

SHAWN: "Well, it's happened to so many others too. It's just something that everybody – "

DR. F: " – Do you get a stomach ache when you..."

SHAWN: "No. It just hurts here. It hurts my heart."

DR. F: "Kind of hard to STOMACH anyway, isn't it? A little organ language."

SHAWN: (I laugh.)

DR. F: "But it's heart BREAKING too."

SHAWN: "Whether she's happy... I don't know where she is now, but..."

DR. F: "You sound like you've really gotten over it."

SHAWN: "I just don't want it to happen again. I guess I'm kind of, well, I was going to say, shell-shocked."

DR. F: "Shell shocked?"

SHAWN: "I guess coming back was... that was a bigger shock than anything."

DR. F: "Coming back from the war?"

SHAWN: "Finding out."

DR. F: "Finding out from the mother?"

I continue to rub my stomach and mutter.

DR. F: "How did you feel at that time?"

SHAWN: "Oh, just awful. I think that's when I started the drinking. I know I drink too much. Between this *(I point to my chest)* and her, it's, I don't know, it's just terrible. I suppose I should not be working in a pub. I know, I can feel it. It's just too much. I shouldn't be doing it."

DR. F: "You can feel it. It would be nice if you could stay with that feeling for a few minutes and see if you can finish it off."

SHAWN: "Well...it's...I guess – "

DR. F: "You guess what?"

SHAWN: "Oh, I don't know. I think I've been using Maggie as an excuse for a long time. To hide from the world."

DR. F: "You don't feel the pain anymore?"

SHAWN: "Not really. I do and I don't, you know. There are times when I do. And I wonder about her sometimes, where she is."

DR. F: "There's a pain I recall you experiencing at that station when she wasn't there – "

SHAWN: " – It was at the ship. At the dock."

DR. F: "The dock? Oh, it was the ship. Okay. When you came off the ship you were in some tremendous pain. How does that feel now?"

I rub the front of my neck back and forth.

SHAWN: "Oh, you know, I wish you'd get off that. I don't want to talk about that anymore."

DR. F: "Okay. That's good. You think you're alright?"

SHAWN: "Well, I think it's about time, don't you think?"

DR. F: "Yeah, I think it's time you were over it. There's a lot of things. If there's any left, you might want to get it out."

I don't respond. I move my head around while I rub the front of my neck.

DR. F: "What's happening, John?"

SHAWN: "Oh, I'm getting hungry... Tomorrow I'll have a good time. I'll just have a little supper and turn in early. It's too cold out anyway. Tomorrow should be better."

DR. F: "It'll be nice and warm tomorrow."

SHAWN: "Should be."

DR. F: "Okay. Let's leave Johnny now."

It took Dr. Field much longer than usual to bring me out of this trance – several minutes. Finally I opened my eyes and began to stir. She asked me some questions to confirm that I was really myself again. My answers were in a very weak voice.

DR. F: "You're speaking so quietly I can hardly hear you. How are you feeling now?"

SHAWN: "Spacey. It was very hard getting back."

DR. F: "Would you like to have stayed at Brighton?"

SHAWN: "Yeah. It was a very strange feeling... I could hear you talking to me, but I was off someplace and I just couldn't get control of myself. I couldn't move. I couldn't open my eyes or talk or anything. I was just sort of off some place. It wasn't unpleasant. It was restful and peaceful. I just felt like I was off in a vacuum somewhere."

DR. F: "You feel rested and peaceful now?"

SHAWN: "Yeah... Like a rag."

DR. F: "I give you the post-hypnotic suggestion, the part of you that is still in trance, that you have a nice, comfortable feeling weekend. If any residue comes up, any interesting dreams or thoughts, like last week when you put yourself in trance, maybe some more of that will happen. If anything comes up, just write it down and put it on the back burner until I get back. You feel okay? If you're not up to driving, just – "

SHAWN: "Oh, I'm getting there. I'm just – "

I make a fluttering movement with my hands. Dr. Field laughs. This concluded the taping.

From the Therapist's Perspective

> *"Clickety clack...clickety clack...*
> *The train goes back...the train goes back...*
> *1994...1993...1980...1960...1920...*
> —Doctor Elly

With Shawn, it was now a continual series of surprises. I used an induction which focused on "comfort".

"I'd like you to become so comfortable — that nothing else matters — except that comfort — a deep sense of peace, weightless suspension. Nothing to think about, nothing to do — except let yourself be — comfortable. And you might begin to feel so comfortable that you sense you're being — all mind without a body, a mind suspended in time and place —."

Subsequently, I deepened his trance state of comfort by having him descend a staircase. "With each step or floor you descend, you go deeper and deeper relaxed." And then I utilized a "train" to take him back in time, a special one car train that travels back in time — a train with a chord above him that he can pull when he wants to "go" and pull again when he wants to stop — a train in which HE is in control. A patient needs to know that he can stop and get off the train at any time, when it might become too uncomfortable for him. Then he can return to a safe place, be it back in the therapy room or a place of comfort he has previously enjoyed.

Could that have promoted the train scene which followed, or would it have come up anyway? John was on a train to Brighton, a place to relax and feel comfortable. I found myself on the train questioning him. When I asked him who he was, it seemed more natural to take on a different identity, as an acquaintance rather than as a therapist. I introduced myself as Sandy, a nickname for my middle name, Sondria. I don't usually involve myself this much in my patients' adventures, but it just seemed right to do so now. Hypnotherapists do go into trance with their patients, and my "trance-sense" told me to take on this role as a therapeutic intervention. The benefit was for me, "as an outsider", to communicate with John in order to learn what he had to offer about his thoughts and feelings.

Shawn's language is an interesting part of this scenario. The lingo is an Irish brogue intermixed with a British accent. Reviewing the video tape of the session, I find it to be awesome, as is the body language which was definitely not Shawn's. It is eerie!

While John spoke about his wound and that of Maggie's having left him, I did my best to get him into some of those devastating feelings in order to utilize what was coming up, as an opportunity to "work through" and release more of the associated emotions. But he did not want to "go there". So I let up, putting that off for another time.

My "comfort" induction seemed to work well. "It was restful and peaceful," he declared at the end of the session. There was a relaxed ambience to the entire train scene. In fact, the parallel between John and Shawn here appears to be that each of them in his own way was seeking comfort and peace, Shawn wanting to be rid of his fear of rainy, windy, gloomy weather, and John wanting a comfortable, peaceful holiday to salve his aching chest and his cold, freezing body.

In fact, I really enjoy reviewing this video. I marvel at Shawn's body language: his shaking, freezing torso, with his arms folded in front of him; his Irish/British lingo which had to be that of John's persona (It was certainly not Shawn's!); and his responses to me, Sandy, including that of his being wounded in the war and that of Maggie's not waiting for him to return — all this, as we traveled together in search of warmth, comfort, and peace.

I concluded the session by suggesting that Shawn do more with this before I see him again— thoughts, dreams, or even more self-trance work — I advised him to write down whatever occurs between this session and our next appointment which was to be in two weeks instead of our usual one. I was leaving for San Francisco to teach one of my ongoing medical hypnosis seminars.

As we departed, little did either one of us know what Mother Nature had in store for us within the next few days. It was as though She might say, "So you're afraid of rainy, windy weather, huh? I'll give you something to really shake your tree!" *And so She did!*

VI

Shaking The Tree

VI

SHAKING THE TREE

*T*he following week was fairly routine. Susan continued to put me off, saying she had to work late. Fearing as I did that our relationship was on the skids, I sent her some flowers. She called and thanked me, but there was something in the sound of her voice. Remember the old song, "Your Lips Tell Me 'No No!' But There's 'Yes Yes' In Your Eyes"? With Susan it was just the opposite. Her lips told me "Yes Yes" but there was "No No" in her tone. We saw each other that weekend, having dinner with some friends before going back to her place. We made love, little knowing that it would be for the last time. As if to bring down the final curtain with a crashing crescendo, it was January 16, only hours before the most terrifying event of my life – the Northridge earthquake.

Even now, years afterwards, it is difficult for me to talk about this monumental catastrophe – indeed, one of the greatest natural disasters in the history of our country. Without going into great detail, let's just say that it was the only time in my life that I was absolutely sure I was going to die.

After the violent shaking finally stopped, I found a flashlight and stumbled through the overturned furniture and debris toward my front door. Outside I could hear many frightened voices, but it was difficult to see where the cries were coming from or how badly damaged the houses in my neighborhood were. The only light was a bloody orange glow in the sky from fires that had broken out several blocks away.

I surveyed my property with my dim flashlight. The two most obvious effects of the quake were the block wall next to my house that had been knocked down and the hot water heater in my garage which was about to tear loose from the wall. Pumped full of adrenalin, I hefted four of the heavy concrete blocks into the garage and wedged them under the platform holding the heater. I may have saved my pipes, but I almost did myself in. I wrenched my back and sent my heart into fibrillation. I became icy cold as my body began to shake almost as hard as the ground had.

It's not clear to me exactly how things happened after that. I recall being in the house next door, trying to call Susan. As her voice came on the phone, I felt myself start to lose consciousness. My neighbor worked for a doctor and could see that I was in pretty bad shape. She grabbed the phone and told Susan she and her husband were taking me to Northridge Emergency Hospital. I think I did pass out for a brief time, because the next thing I remember is lying in the chaotic hospital emergency ward, being given injections. My heart continued to beat erratically for a couple of hours before it settled back to a normal rhythm. Then, because none of the elevators was working, several attendants carried me up two flights of stairs to a hospital room.

Shortly thereafter, Susan appeared at my door. She quickly convinced me that Northridge Hospital, with no plumbing and no power, was the last place in the world to be. She got me to her car and drove me to her place.

I stayed with Susan for the next three days. The San Fernando Valley was a shambles, as was much of Santa Monica and many other parts of Los Angeles. Several freeways had collapsed and electricity was out everywhere. Thousands of homes and businesses were virtually destroyed. Fortunately, because of the early morning hour when the quake hit, there were many fewer fatalities than would have occurred just an hour or two later. And yet, Susan's area was almost untouched. I was amazed to discover that nothing had even fallen off a shelf in her condo.

During my time at her place Susan was thoughtful, kind, considerate... and very cool. Rather than her lover, I felt like a burdensome old uncle with a bad back and a tricky ticker. I'm sure she wasn't trying to make me feel like a drudge, but like myself, Susan wasn't much good at hiding her true feelings. Four days later power was finally restored to my area. Susan helped me straighten up my house, then left me to fend for myself. As soon as her car disappeared from view, we had an aftershock. And they kept coming every few hours. I felt a little foolish sleeping in my clothes on the sofa that night, but I found out later that most people I knew were doing the same thing.

The next day I stopped by my doctor's office and had him check me over. My back was much better and my heart was okay. He refilled my anti-fibrillation prescription and sent me on my way. The pharmacist had trouble locating my medication – the drugstore was in total disarray.

I didn't see Susan that weekend. I figured she'd had enough of me during the past few days. Most of my friends sustained much more serious damage than I did. My boss and his wife had suffered a total loss of their home. There were several more aftershocks on Saturday – small ones to be sure, but I don't care who you are, when the ground is jumping around under your feet, it's upsetting, to say the least. Sunday was quiet, that is, until evening. Then the tremblers got bigger and more frequent. Around ten o'clock there were four of them, quite close together, all measuring more than 4.0 on the Richter Scale. It was enough to get my juices flowing fast and hard. I admit I was very frightened.

I called Susan. I wondered if she'd felt the shakers. She'd just gone to bed and hadn't noticed anything. Then I did the unforgivable. I asked if I could come over and spend the night. There was a long pause, then a very flat, "Oh, okay." That should've been the tipoff. But being as shaken (literally) as I was, I ignored the obvious. The expression on her face when she opened her door said it all. I was as welcome as an IRS auditor. I said to her, "You don't want me here, do you?" She replied, very flatly, "Oh, you can stay... if you want to." I didn't reply. I just turned and walked out. The next few days melted into a big hopeless, shapeless blob. I can't remember a time when I felt lower. With all the misery so many others were suffering, it was a true living nightmare. The aftershocks kept coming and just to top things off, it rained. I have to admit that there were a few moments when the word "suicide" slogged through my mind. I had to get away from this morbid mess.

I flew up to Vancouver, Washington to visit my brother Bill. He was very busy as Head of the English Department at a Community College, but was good enough to take a few days off to help me get my act together. Just being able to talk things out with him was immensely helpful. And, for the first time in many days, I was able to get a good night's sleep.

I was beginning to feel a lot better when I returned to Los Angeles a few days later. But the ride from the airport back to my house brought me down pretty hard. All along the route there were signs of the recent disaster – condemned buildings, broken windows, cracks in the freeway, yellow tape everywhere. And it was raining again.

When I got home, I checked my answering machine, thinking Susan might possibly have called. I had several messages from friends, complimenting me on a recent article I'd written on animation that appeared in the Los Angeles Times while I was away. But nothing from Susan. I was relieved she hadn't phoned. It made it easier for me to face the music.

I tried to do some writing in the late afternoon, but a power failure hit and wiped out all my work. The lights were off for over an hour. I began to think again of moving away from L.A. for good. I even called my brother to see if there were any condos in his area for sale.

The next day I saw Dr. Field for the first time since the earthquake. We commiserated about our experiences. She'd been in San Francisco during the quake, but returned to a severely damaged house and was in the midst of major repairs. Then I brought up Susan and how we'd split up. Dr. Field suggested that I waste no time in starting to see other women. I reacted negatively to that, feeling in no mood for any female companionship. As a matter of fact, I was pretty negative about everything – especially my therapy. What was I getting out of it? I'd lost my girl friend; I was anxious all the time and I was still spooked by wind and rain. Picking up on my frustration, Dr. Field suggested that we resume our past life regressions. She felt there was a great deal to be learned that would help my present day situation. I didn't see the connection, but, if for no other reason than to have a little escape from the here and now, I agreed to go back and revisit the life and times of John Williams.

Dr. Field put me through the standard relaxation exercise and again got me onto a train moving back in time. Once more it was the express to Brighton that I, as John, had ridden during the last session. The trip ended quickly and I was soon in my hotel.

"What part of the hotel are you in now?" asked Dr. Field.

"The dining room... Thank you."

"Thank you?"

"I was thanking the maitre d'. He's showing me to my table. It's by the window."

I could see the ocean and the pebble beach, all in different shades of grey. The sky was overcast and it started to sprinkle. I began to feel quite sad as I looked around outside. The only person about was an old man walking along the road adjoining the hotel, his white beard flowing in the wind. He held his hat on with the handle of his walking stick. Then I scanned the dining room. There were only three or four others seated. This was indeed a lonely holiday. I took out a locket with Maggie's picture that I always carried with me. Don't ask me why I did that because every time I looked at her beautiful face it made me very melancholy. I motioned to the waiter and ordered a large whiskey. I quickly downed it and ordered another. But my feelings of gloom only deepened. I started to think about cutting my vacation short and returning home.

I then went into a kind of empty state for a few moments, as if floating in a vast nowhere. Dr. Field patiently waited for me to move on. I was again sitting at a table with a drink in my hand. But now I was in a different place – it was the Red Dog, my regular pub.

"What year is it, John?" Dr. Field asked.

"1924."

"Four years later?"

"Yeah."

I raised my glass up and looked toward Molly, the barmaid. "Again, Molly!"

Molly brought me the drink, then asked me to play something. I always acted reluctant, enjoying the coaxing from Molly and the others. I quickly downed my whiskey and nipped over to the old upright piano as everyone called out their favorites: "Play 'Knees Up, Mother Brown'! Let's have 'Old Dutch'! How about 'The Old Kent Road'! Play 'By The Seaside'!" I decided I was going to do a popular song from the states – "Yes, We Have No Bananas." I sang a chorus and then the others joined in. It was great fun.

Then I was on a stage. A small orchestra was playing a bouncy tune and people were cheering. I was doing a really silly dance step I'd learned from a soldier who'd been a circus clown before the war. Now I was performing it on amateur night at a music hall. I'd done this before. I finished up with a kind of semi pratfall. People threw coins on the stage and cheered. I took fast bows as I scooped up all the coins.

But then everything switched. I suddenly felt very down.

"What's happening now?" asked Dr. Field.

"I don't know. I have a headache."

"Where are you?"

I looked around. I was sitting on the edge of a bed. The only light was from a small bedside table lamp. I was dressed, but my coat was off and my shirt was open. Then Molly entered the room, wearing a bathrobe. She had a glass in her hand. She handed it to me. I didn't want it. I'd already had too much to drink. She said it was only a fizz-water and it would make me feel better. I drank it down. Molly then sat down on the bed beside me and put her arm around my shoulder.

Dr. Field said, "You're frowning and shaking your head. What's going on?"

"Oh, Molly's starting in on me again."

"What do you mean, 'Starting in'?"

"Oh, she's always after me to get a divorce so she and I can get married. She says I need someone to take care of me."

"How do you feel about that?"

"Bloody awful!"

I got very sick to my stomach. I probably would have made a mess on Dr. Field's floor if she hadn't quickly interceded, giving me a suggestion that my stomach was okay. But my head still felt woozy. Meantime, Molly was talking a blue streak.

"Ah, geez!" I cried out.

"Now what's the matter?" asked Dr. Field.

"She's on me again for my drinking. Imagine that, would you? A barmaid giving a man a hard time for using her services. Well, I don't want to hear it."

I was in no mood for criticism. I staggered to my feet and left Molly's place in a drunken huff.

After a moment, I found myself walking across the Tower Bridge in London. It was nearing dawn. There was a heavy layer of mist hanging over the river. I stopped and looked down and wondered how it would feel if I jumped into that fog cloud. Maybe it would be like falling into meringue or cotton candy. It seemed as though I came to this particular place a lot and thought a good deal about ending it all. Of course I never really would. I'd had a strict Catholic upbringing and even the thought of suicide was a sin – albeit a forgivable one. But suicide itself was a one-way ticket to damnation. And yet, so much of the time, especially when I wasn't drinking, I felt like I was already in hell. Once more I took out the locket and looked at Maggie's picture. Then I continued on my way.

Dr. Field now suggested that I move ahead in time. I went into a neutral state for a few moments, then I was walking on a train station platform. I could feel the wooden planks creaking under my footsteps.

"What year is it?" Dr. Field asked.

"1935. It's summer time."

As before with Molly, I felt queasy and a bit shaky. The midday sun was beating down, making me uncomfortably hot and sweaty. I took off my hat and wiped the brim with my handkerchief. Then I moved closer to the platform's edge and looked down the track, trying to see if my train was coming. I wanted a drink very badly. I pulled a flask out of my pocket, but it was empty. Then I got dizzy. Everything was spinning. I reached out to lean against a post, but missed it. I lost my balance and fell off the platform to the tracks several feet below. My head struck one of the rails. Then I was above my body, looking down. I could see myself sprawled across the tracks. My figure got smaller and smaller, as if I were moving up and away from it. Then everything went dark. I was sure I had died.

From the Therapist's Perspective

"Having responded to his own call and continuing to follow courageously as the consequences unfold, the hero finds all the forces of the unconscious at his side. Mother Nature herself supports the mighty task. And in so far as the hero's act coincides with that for which his society itself is ready, he seems to ride on the great rhythm of the historical process."
—Joseph Campbell, *Hero with a Thousand Faces*

"Mirror, mirror on the wall...
Were you among the first to fall?"
—Doctor Elly

8:00 AM - South San Francisco

I am suddenly jarred awake by the incessant ringing of the alarm clock. 'Day Two of the medical hypnosis seminar I am presenting, starting at 10:00 AM. I peer out through the large curved window which faces the bed in my hotel suite. The San Mateo Bridge sparkles in the sunlight which streams through the half-drawn drape. I decide to turn over and grab another forty winks.

Drifting off again, I hear the phone. Boris drops his razor and hurries to answer it. He tells me it's one of my psychologist students.

"I hate to be the bearer of bad news," declares the voice, "but there's been a huge earthquake in L.A. ...epicenter in a place called Northridge."

The voice continues, "Turn on the TV!"

I grab the remote! My first thoughts are of my elderly father who lives in Santa Monica. A queasy feeling enters my stomach. I wonder about my home, my office. And there is my patient Shawn. He hates rain and wind; how will he cope with an earthquake? CNN is showing scenes from Encino where my home is, in the Santa Monica mountains bordering the San Fernando Valley.

Several houses have slipped down a hill! The scene shifts quickly to other disaster areas - severely damaged apartments in Woodland Hills, Studio City, Reseda and Northridge, and a new office building in West Los Angeles - at least twenty miles from the epicenter. People are being rescued from the wreckage! Some hospitals are evacuating their patients and others are overloaded, understaffed, and working without water, lights, and power!

Boris heads for home without delay. In the meantime, I begin teaching Day Two as the "show must go on". With every break, I leave the conference area and return to my room and the CNN station that was not to be turned off for the rest of my stay. It becomes my refuge, my only support, my night light, and my day light. I dial the phone persistently — wanting to reach someone in L.A. — my father, a friend, a colleague, my father's next door neighbor, and after many hours, Boris. Even the operator makes a special effort for me, but to no avail.

My seminar lasts its usual five days. As the L.A. phone service is restored, I finally manage to reach my father and my husband. Dad's apartment building had some structural damage, but thankfully he is unhurt. As for our home, Boris reports that the ornamental blocks on the wall around the pool appear to be the only major structural casualty. His description of the damage to the inside of our house was a bit more daunting. He describes it as if all the contents had been put into a dice cup, shaken around and then dumped out. The interior of our office was in a similar state.

I also heard from Boris that Shawn wants a session with me by telephone. The thought comes to me that I have been gone at a time when Shawn might have needed his therapist the most. Shawn sounds terrible. He relays his quake experiences to me, including the many after-shocks, the heart fibrillation, and the problems at Northridge Hospital Medical Center, as well as his adventures with Susan, who is rapidly leaping out of his life. His visit to his brother provided some short-lived relief.

A few days later I returned to L.A and saw Shawn in my office. Heavy rain could be seen from the large picture windows. The sound of the tremendous downpour was anything but pleasant.

Emotionally, Shawn was in an especially bad place. He looked as gloomy as the weather. He did not respond well to my relaxation suggestions, so I thought we might alleviate some of his anxiety and depression by once more going back to his *other life*. Again, utilizing the train that travels back in time, Shawn, as John Williams, returned to that same hotel in Brighton. It was a sad scene, mimicking the present – a windy, rainy panorama viewed from his hotel dining room window. That and gazing at a picture of his estranged wife Maggie made him feel very melancholy. He tried to drown his sorrows in the whiskey he ordered.

However, John perked up when the scene changed, first to his regular pub where he was happily playing the piano, and then to an English Music Hall where he was performing a "silly dance" for a delighted amateur night crowd. But then he slipped once more into a melancholy state.

Molly was soothing his drunken, sick self in her bedroom while exhorting him to get a divorce and marry her. As the day dawned, he saw himself at the Tower Bridge where he fantasized jumping into the cloud of fog that covered the river below. And so, a suicide theme becomes a part of this complex picture.

I suggested he move ahead in time. It was 1935, and John was on a train platform. He again felt queasy and shaky. He lost his balance and fell off the platform to the tracks several feet below, his head hitting a rail. John reported leaving his body, rising above, and looking down at himself sprawled across the tracks. As all became dark, he was certain that he had died. This scene evolved in Shawn's first therapy session subsequent to the quake.

As a result of the quake, Shawn's heart had gone into fibrillation to such an extent that he indeed thought he was in danger of dying. In our telephone conversation he had told me how he had become icy cold while his body "shook like the ground". He had actually lost consciousness for a time in the E.R.

Was he also not conscious about what was happening between him and Susan? Shawn was really in denial about that one. It was obvious to me, but not to him, that their relationship was over. I was concerned about his reaction to that disappointment.

At the time, I was not sure where the session had led us. Shawn's mood paralleled John's – sad, gloomy, down and out, melancholy. And when, Shawn, in this life, thought he was surely going to die, John, in the other life, actually does. John had been so glad to survive the wound in the war, and yet with his prior hint of suicidal behavior, he brought on his own death by falling from the train platform.

What could all this mean for Shawn today? He was still going through the hell of the earthquake and its aftershocks, as were countless others who were severely traumatized by this cataclysmic event. Indeed, my workload increased dramatically as so many people were reporting all kinds of new symptoms related to the quake, such as extreme anxiety and inability to sleep. For Shawn, his already present phobias were being put to a test that was devastating. Instead of unraveling, the situation was becoming more complex — with loss, death and destruction hanging like a black cloud over this time and the past.

VII

Abandoned

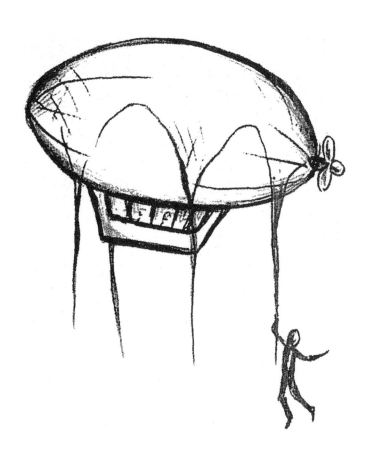

VII

ABANDONED

he experience of "dying" under hypnosis was, needless to say, a jarring one. For several hours after I left Dr. Field's office, the image of my own body lying face down on that track haunted my mind. What a pitiful ending to a sad, short life. It was only later as I got ready for bed that it occurred to me to do some mental calculating. This event had happened at the hottest time of the year – July or August of 1935. Since I was born in April of 1936, that meant there had been just about nine months between John Williams' death and Shawn Regan's birth. If one believes in the transmigration of souls, I'd say that was pretty neat scheduling.

The next few days I thought hard and long about all this John Williams stuff – From the time I'd had the bayoneting experience I'd been bouncing back and forth on the subject of reincarnation. Did I or did I not really live and die before? And if I didn't, why would I make up such a miserable existence? Why would I want to have been such a weak-willed, alcoholic loser? I didn't like John Williams and I hated the life he'd led. But real or imaginary, he was a part of me. I began to realize that sooner or later I'd have to make a serious archival search for John, to see if I could find out if he had been an actual person or just a bizarre figment of my imagination. Meantime, life went on. My fear of wind and rain seemed to diminish, but only because the earthquake and its after effects were so much more upsetting. Intermittent after-shocks, which always seemed to hit at four in the morning, kept me and just about everyone else in Los Angeles on edge. I continued sleeping with my pants at the foot of the bed and using the TV as a night light.

And I was at a terrible stage with Susan. I felt like the guy I'd seen in an old newsreel film who, along with several others, was trying to tether a dirigible. Suddenly the wind came up and the big airship rose sharply. Everybody except this one tenacious dude let go. He hung on until he was about a hundred feet off the ground. Then he lost his grip and down he went. I knew that the longer I hung onto Susan, the harder I'd fall. But I just couldn't let go yet.

Valentine's Day came and I sent her a huge flower arrangement. This brought a phoned thank you. But no indication that she wanted to see me. I called her a couple more times in the next few days, but she just killed me with cordiality. The message was clear. Thanks, but no thanks. And have a nice day. I was so bummed out that by the time I next saw Dr. Field, I literally ached all over. My jaw was so tight I could have opened soup cans with my teeth. And my back was stiffer than yesterday's bubble gum. Dr. Field tried to help me with some hypnotic relaxation techniques, but instead of letting go of my body's tension, I once again slipped back into the identity of John Williams. And, far from feeling any relief, the tension in my body turned into pain and a feeling of dizziness. I began to squirm and groan. Obviously, this was not what Dr. Field had intended.

"What's happening, Shawn?"

As had happened before, I didn't respond to the name "Shawn" when I was in my John Williams persona. I just grunted incoherently as I looked around and tried to focus my eyes. I was lying on a floor in a bar. My jaw felt like someone had just slugged me. Then I looked up and saw Molly standing over me.

"Where did he go?" I blurted out.

"Where did who go?" asked Dr. Field.

"I'm talking to Molly!" I snapped. Molly didn't answer me. She just bent over and mopped my forehead with a wet bar towel. Again I asked her, "Where is he? Where's the bloke who bashed me? I'll break his bloody arse."

Molly told me that nobody had struck me, that I'd stumbled in drunk and fallen on my face. She propped me up and put the rolled up towel under my neck. As I lay on the floor, even though nobody had laid a glove on me, I felt beat up and embarrassed. I started to sob. Dr. Field very patiently let me cry for a minute or two, then she gave me the suggestion that I would gather myself together and that my pain would diminish. As soon I settled down, I started relating to her where I was and what was happening.

"What year is it, John?" she asked.

"1928. Oh, poor Molly. The dear woman's fed up with my drinking. And, I don't blame her."

"But she works in the bar, doesn't she?"

"Yeah, but she won't serve me anymore. I do most of my drinking across the road now. I just come in at closing time to take her home."

"Do you live together?"

"I got my own digs, but we spend most nights together. At least until lately. She won't let me in when I'm spiffed."

"And is that often?"

"About every night. I know what you're going to say – why don't I quit the drinking, right? Well, I try. I honest to God really try. Oh, I can go a day or two without the stuff, but then I start wanting to jump off bridges. I'm like my father. He always said he was born two drinks short. And so was I."

"Your father? I don't believe you've ever mentioned him before."

"Well, to be honest... I made him up."

"Made him up?"

"Yeah. When I was a kid in the orphanage all of us made up fantasy parents. I guess I just kept mine a little longer than most."

"So you were an orphan?"

"Not really. My Old Man ran off when my brother and I were just little tykes. Mum tried to raise us by herself, but she couldn't handle it, so she put us in St. Stebben's."

"St. Stebben's?"

"It was actually called, 'St. Stephen's', but everybody called it 'St. Stebben's'. It was a Catholic orphan school."

"Where was it located?"

"I'm not sure. Kent, maybe. Somewhere outside the city."

Dr. Field asked if I'd like to go back to my childhood at the school. I began to feel very sad.

"No. I'd rather not."

"Do you feel that your parents abandoned you?"

"Please. Let's get off this. I don't want to talk about it."

Dr. Field didn't press me any further. Instead, she slowly brought me back to the present, again suggesting that my aches and pains be eliminated and that I would feel relaxed. When I opened my eyes, my jaw and back were pretty loose, but I still felt very low. We'd really touched a nerve when John Williams' childhood came up.

At the end of the session, Dr. Field once again put me in trance and gave me a post-hypnotic suggestion that I could bring up more information from my previous life on my own, using self-hypnosis. She felt that there were a great many important details there that related to my hot button issue of abandonment. It was the thread that ran through everything from my fear of bad weather to my difficulty relating to a woman...a tangle of rope that tied me up in knots and was taking the joy out of my life just as it had taken the joy out of the life of John Williams. The next day, I set aside some quiet time to explore my alter-ego's past. I sat down in my favorite chair (The one with duct tape on the arm rest, a la Frazier Crane's father's chair) and used the self-hypnosis technique Dr. Field had taught me, reassuring myself as I went under that if something very painful or threatening came up, I could always escape back to the safety of the present merely by tapping my finger.

I closed my eyes, and slowly drifted back to another time. I felt very sad and was crying. So was my brother. We were just little kids; I was about seven or eight and my brother four or five. We were saying goodbye to our mother. There was a nun and a priest there. We were standing by the big iron gate outside a large gray stone building. My mother tells us that everything will be alright, that she'll come and see us in a few days.

Then it was night. Carley (*My brother. I believe his given name was Charles, but he was always called "Carley" instead of "Charley".*) and I were in bed. It was several weeks later.

Carley and I talked about our mother and how we hadn't seen her for so long. We tried to reassure each other that she'd be coming back soon.

Then it was daytime and I was in the yard outside the big stone building with some other boys. We were talking about the girls in the school. There was a group of smaller buildings behind the big main one and the young girls were boarded there. They didn't let us boys play with them. We pretended not to care much, but we were all curious about them, far more curious than we would have been if we'd spent much time together.

Then we started talking about our parents. As I mentioned earlier, we all made up stories about our mothers and fathers, most of whom nobody had ever really known, and why they didn't come to see us. I concocted a real whopper about my father – he was a secret government agent on a spy mission in Europe. The whole school would be in mortal danger if he came to see my brother and me, so he communicated with us in code. I'd pick out a personal ad in the newspaper and tell everyone that my father put it there just for my benefit. Then I'd "decode" its secret meaning. I thought I was very clever, but I don't think I fooled anyone. We all knew each others' tales were made up, but we never let on because it helped us cope.

The scene suddenly changed. Time moved ahead a couple of years. I became aware of a faint scent of lavender and I heard a melody being played haltingly on a piano. The sound grew louder, and then I realized that I was the one playing. I could see the keys, which seemed large for my fingers. And, there was sheet music propped up in front of me. My feet barely reached the pedals. "Very good. Very good," someone said. I turned and there was a nun in a black habit sitting next to me on the bench. She was very pretty, especially for a sister. Sister Veronica was her name. And I had a crush on her. She was sitting close enough to me that I could feel warmth from her body. That body heat, her lavender scent and her lovely, kind face were a real turn-on for a boy of ten. I always looked forward to our piano lessons, not so much because I loved music, but because I was in love with Sister Veronica. But not as a substitute mother. I felt a kind of blooming lust as I fantasized about what she looked like without that black habit.

The lesson was over for the day, but I tried to drag it out. I asked her if I could do my piece over but she said no. Then I did something very daring – something I'd always wondered about. I asked Sister Veronica what color her hair was. As soon as the words were out of my mouth, I felt like I'd done something very naughty. But she wasn't at all upset. She smiled, then pulled back her hood, revealing a generous amount of light brown hair. It was very erotic, or as erotic as anything can be to a ten year old. I started to have an erection. It was very embarrassing. I jumped off the bench and ran out of the room so she couldn't see it.

That was all I could glean that day, but before my next appointment with Dr. Field, I continued to use this self-hypnotic technique to bring up more details of John Williams' early life. However, it didn't work every time. I was having a lot of trouble concentrating during this period because of my preoccupation with Susan and the more than occasional aftershock. So it wasn't always possible to get myself into a relaxed enough state to induce a trance.

But when I was able to let go, I discovered a few more things, like the fact that after I'd been at St. Stebbens' for a year or so, I'd overheard two of the nuns talking about my mother. She had apparently left the country. This was actually a relief because for some time up until then I believed she had died. It was better to have a live mother than a dead one, even though I hated her for deserting my brother and me.

We all feared and at the same time looked forward to the day when we'd leave the school and get out into the real world. There were scholarships available for the very brightest of us to go onto upper school. But the majority were usually apprenticed out to some tradesman or business. We heard horror stories of how some of the lads had been terribly abused by their masters, made to slave long hours for little or no money. But I was very fortunate. When I was twelve I was taken in by a master bootmaker named Moseby Conyers. He was getting up in years and needed someone to help him in his London shop. I tried to have him take Carley too, but he was too young and Mose only needed one apprentice. Carley and I had a tearful parting and promised to stay in touch, but I couldn't recall what became of him. It's possible I never saw him again.

As sad as I was to leave, I soon grew very fond of Mose and his wife. They were very nice people and treated me like a son. I lived with them in their flat over Mose's London shop as I learned my trade. Mose was a real craftsman and made very good shoes and boots. He had some very wealthy customers. I could see Mose and myself in our aprons working over a bench in the back of the shop. I loved the feel of the leather and the tools and the smell of the workshop. Meantime his wife (Everybody called her "Mumzie") waited on our clientele. She had a very sweet way about her and was especially good at handling dissatisfied customers.

Mose was not a hard drinking man, but he liked to pop over to the Blue Boar after work and have a pint before supper. It was pretty much his only social life and it was his one chance during the day to get out of the shop. He would take me along, although I was only allowed to have ginger beer or something else non-alcoholic. But that was okay. The Blue Boar was not just a place for adults to drink. Women and well behaved kids were also welcome. I was treated really well, especially when I sat down at the piano and played a few popular tunes. (Thank you, Sister Veronica.) I especially liked the attention I got from women, but they were all too old for me and there was never any opportunity for fun and games. I wouldn't have had any idea what to do even if there had been.

When I reached eighteen, I was getting restless, as any young man would, to get out and see the world. But I had a good trade and a secure job so I was really torn, especially because I felt I owed Mose so much. How could I leave without letting him and Mumzie down? The outbreak of the war in Europe seemed a perfect opportunity to have it both ways. Like so many other young Brits, I was full of patriotic zeal and anxious to do my bit for my country, which only intensified my desire to get away. So I volunteered for the army. Mose was, of course, very upset with me. He wasn't getting any younger and he relied on me more and more. But I assured him, as the government was telling us, that the war would be over in a matter of weeks or months. I'd be back before he knew it. Reluctantly, Mose and Mumzie gave me their blessing and off I went.

I did my basic training at the big army base at Leeds. While the program they put us through was physically grueling, the morale was very high. We were all volunteers and anxious to fight for King and country and to get into action. Every one of us was sure he'd come back dripping with medals because Englishmen were obviously superior to everyone else, especially the "Bosch" as we called the Germans. We had no idea how naive we were about what war really meant.

About the time I finished my basic training, I met Maggie. I'd seen her a few times because she used to ride along with her father on his wagon. He was a dairy farmer and delivered milk and eggs to the base. But I didn't actually get to know her until I met her in town one day. She surprised me by inviting me up to her house for dinner.

I hit it off with her old man right away when I told him I was a shoemaker. He was too, at least he had been, but now the only shoes he made were for horses. Her mother was something else. Very quiet and never smiled.

Maggie and I had a whirlwind courtship. We only saw each other a few times before I got my orders to ship out. It was about here that it started to get more and more difficult to recall events clearly. I couldn't visualize our wedding or any honeymoon we might have had. All I know is that it was a very sudden decision and that I'd had very little time with her as Mrs. John Williams before I left for the war. The last image I had was of a painfully sad farewell at the troop ship.

From this point on, all further attempts to bring back information on my own about John Williams were futile. Why that was, I couldn't say for sure – maybe the post-hypnotic suggestion that I could do it had worn off, or maybe the next phase of John's life, the war years, was too tough to deal with.

In any event, I couldn't wait to see Dr. Field again, not only to report to her what I had discovered, but just to have someone to talk to. I wasn't discussing anything with anybody about delving into a possible past life and it was like walking around with a huge undigested meal in my stomach. I really needed to get it out. Meantime, the obstruction in my gut found its way to my head. I developed a king-sized case of writers' block. In addition to an assignment for the studio, I'd been working on two other projects of my own. But during these few days in between sessions with Dr. Field, all I could do was sit at my keyboard and stare at a blank screen. Creatively, I was out to lunch.

From the Therapist's Perspective

"What lies behind us and what lies before us
are tiny matters compared to what lies within us."
—Oliver Wendell Holmes

As Shawn's therapist, and observer of his experiencing that other life, I marveled at his report of the nine month differential between John's death and Shawn's birth. More and more about his escapades as John Williams appeared to be right on. Our sessions together often seemed to begin with "Believe It Or Not".

As I stated before, previous to Shawn's experience, I had never believed in past lives. Now I was becoming more and more of a believer. So much of the laundry of Shawn's present life appeared to hang on the clothes line of John Williams. And now, a nine month separation between the death of John and the birth of Shawn! Incredible!

Meanwhile, in this life, Los Angeles, and especially the San Fernando Valley, kept experiencing the rock and roll of the Big One's aftershocks. And so Shawn believed his fear of rain and wind diminished only because he was being subjected to something worse. I don't think so. I believe his fear of rainy, windy weather was indeed diminishing and had been doing so, ever so slowly as phobias will, since the episode of John Williams' being bayoneted in the trenches in a total misery of wind and rain. Like many patients who dislike *change* because they are fearful of "what next?", Shawn wanted to believe his phobia was as intact as ever. *Letting go* means what do I do with the energy previously wrapped up in all that stuff? How do I go about my day now? It's tough starting a new life without the old habits. It's like an alcoholic wondering what to do with the time he used to spend at the bar, or the time which he had spent at home rolling around a glass in his hand, while enjoying the tinkling sound of the ice cubes. Or, to take that one step further, the time he spent zonked out, drunk and avoiding life.

At our next session, Shawn expressed how upset he was about his relationship with Susan. I attempted to relax his body and mind with hypnosis. But Shawn went "back there" again. Then I made the ultimate mistake of calling him "Shawn", not knowing that his body movements were once more that of John. John was into a drunken binge and Molly was rescuing him. As he began to cry, I had him focus in on the feelings he was experiencing, the bodily sensations, and to stay with the release of those feelings for a good while. It was much longer than the "minute or two" which Shawn recalls. Time distortion is one of the basic phenomena of hypnosis, and what seems like only a moment in trance can be a lot longer. It was my theory that if John released *fully* with his tears, that which *HE* was experiencing in that time, Shawn would also be through with what those related feelings were about.

Venting feelings is the essence of "letting go". I believed that if John let go of the aches and pains involved with that drunken binge, that its corollary in this life, whatever that was, would also be complete. Could that related part be the pain Shawn was experiencing because of the curtain coming down on his relationship with Susan? Could John's feelings of having been "beaten up and embarrassed" also relate to Shawn's present feelings and thoughts about his closure with Susan? When John had completed his release or "catharsis", as the term goes, I added verbally that he would let go of the pain and move on. I said something to him about his gathering himself together, which I anticipated would apply to the Shawn and Susan situation, as well. For sure, Shawn had fallen on his face with her, like drunken John had when in front of Molly. And now it was time for Shawn to put it all together and move on. I repeated the suggestion that he *would now let go of the pain*.

As John continued describing the events of his life, he went back to his childhood traumas, that of the abandonment by his father and then by his mother. John reported that he and his brother Carly were sent to an orphanage, where they both remained for much of their formative years. He did not talk about abandonment per se, but it obviously added up to that. I wanted John to return to that earlier part of his life but he did not want to do so. Abandonment seemed to be a theme related to both Shawn and John — from John's mother, and later, his wife Maggie — to Shawn's mother and now, the loss of his latest love, Susan. I sensed it was more than coincidence which caused the St. Stebbens story to unravel that day.

Before we ended that session, I did some further trance work with Shawn where I gave him the post-hypnotic suggestion that he use self-hypnosis between sessions and further explore other events in the life of John Williams. As he reported in the following session, he did do some incredible work on his own. Shawn had some fascinating revelations of John's orphanage years, from the little lad who created tales about the secret agent Dad he never knew, to his love for "unavailable Sister Veronica," the nun who taught him the piano, through to his years with the bootmaker, Mose. John's description of his departure from his brother added more to the abandonment theme, as did his taking leave from Mose to join the armed forces. Finally, it was John's painfully sad farewell to Maggie, the Mrs. John Williams he hardly knew and would never see again, that completed the picture of abandonment. Thus, on his own, Shawn had reconstructed some of the most significant events in the life and times of John Williams — and maybe, symbolically...in the life and times of Shawn Regan.

VIII

"It Ain't Gonna Rain No Mo"

VIII

"IT AIN'T GONNA RAIN NO MO"

*A*nd so it went until my next appointment. For those few days, I felt like I'd had a lobotomy. And to make matters worse, there was increased pressure on me to get work out. Besides the two projects of my own and the cartoon script I was doing, a publisher, who had a partially completed book of mine, but whom I hadn't heard from for weeks, called suddenly and asked for another chapter as fast as I could get it to him. How did I respond? I got right to work staring at a blank screen again. I started to crave a smoke, even though I'd sworn off tobacco fifteen years earlier. Then I began thinking of other things I needed to get done, like folding my underwear, cleaning the crumbs out from under my toaster and checking out the glove compartment of my car for old gum. I fit perfectly Robert Benchley's classic definition of a writer — someone who sits down to the keyboard and prays for the phone to ring. Since no one was calling, I decided to get on the phone and bother my friends. And wouldn't you know? I "accidentally" dialed Susan. I really meant to call an animator buddy of mine, but my hot little fingers, starved for instructions from my brain, were working on their own.

Susan was almost as surprised as I was that I'd phoned. She had to cut me off quickly because she was packing to go to Japan. Her company was sending her there to supervise the filming of a commercial. So, there was just time to say "bye bye" and "bon voyage".

What a jerk! Why couldn't I just read the handwriting on the wall and end it?

My next appointment with Dr. Field finally rolled around and I had lots to tell her, especially about all the information I'd gotten on my own about John Williams. I actually brought along notes that I'd made, so I wouldn't forget anything. I went over all the material in detail, and even though she is always professional and level headed, Dr. Field couldn't help expressing her excitement that I'd been able to recapture so much from my "other life".

But remarkable as all this past life activity was, I was much more interested in dealing with the here and now. I was terribly bothered by my general "deer in the headlights" state of inertia. I was creatively constipated; I was still "stuck on" Susan; I was still immobilized by wind and rain. Even though it had been fairly mild, just the thought of bad weather would rattle me. I was constantly up tight because of all of the aftershocks. Dr. Field dealt with the last problem first. Everybody was tense about the tremors, she reminded me. You'd have to be insane not to be. Concerning my weather demon, that would have to wait for another test; however, she was confident that I'd hold up much better the next time we had a storm. As far as being stuck on Susan, Dr. Field again urged me to get out and date other women. We went around and around on that one. I was still resisting any new romantic endeavors with a passion. And when Dr. Field suggested that I try a dating service, I blew. "No way! That's for losers! Forget it! End of story!"

"Okay. We'll pass on that for now. So what about this "creative constipation"? What's that all about?"

"That's exactly what it is. I can't get anything out."

"You know, Shawn, you've complained about this off and on as long as I've known you. And yet you always seem to work your way out of it."

"But this is different. I really feel like there's a big rock stuck in my brain."

"Alright, how would you like to try some hypnosis to get at

the root of this blockage?"

I agreed and she guided me back to my own youth. I was twelve years old and just getting interested in girls, but I didn't know exactly why. Believe it or not, I still had no idea that men and women had intercourse. I know it's hard to swallow that today, but remember, this was back around 1950 when you couldn't even say the word "pregnant" on radio or TV. And, I'd been raised in a Catholic school where they were especially adept at keeping anything that might be pleasurable away from their charges.

"Where are you now?" the doctor asked.

"In my bedroom. I'm drawing."

"What are you drawing?"

"A girl in a magazine. I'm copying her picture. She's got on a bathing suit, but..."

"But what?"

"I'm drawing her without it. Oh, oh..."

"What's the matter?"

"I think I hear my mother coming. I better hide this in the book case."

"You like to draw?"

"Oh, yeah. Especially sports stuff. And... you know."

"Girls without their clothes on?"

"Yeah. But I think it's wrong."

"Wrong?"

"Yeah. You're not supposed to do stuff like this. My mother would kill me if she ever saw these pictures."

Dr. Field and I talked a bit more about how confused and uninformed I was about sex. Then time seemed to move ahead a few days. I'd been out playing baseball with my friends and had just come home for lunch. I walked into my bedroom and there was my mother, sitting on the edge of my bed with my drawings in her hand. The angry expression on her face was terrifying. She tore me to pieces, telling me what a dirty kid I was and how disappointed she was in me. Then she gave me the "Wait till your father gets home" routine. That was the most miserable afternoon of my life. I felt like a dead-kid-walking as I waited for my dad to arrive and do God knows what to me. When he finally came into my room and confronted me, I was so scared and ashamed I couldn't talk. I was surprised at how low key he was. He said very little about the whole thing and told me I had to go see the priest the next day, Saturday, when they heard confessions.

Time moved forward to the following afternoon. I was walking around the block past our church, my heart beating like a hundred drums. I don't know how many times I passed by St. Mark's before I finally went inside. When I finally got up the courage to enter the confessional, I stammered so much the priest told me he couldn't understand what I was saying. After several jumbled attempts to communicate to him what happened, I think he got the gist of it. I gritted my teeth in anticipation of a stern tongue lashing. But like my dad, the priest was very non-judgmental. He didn't lecture me or anything, but just gave me a rosary to say for a penance.

Then I was home, my dad asking me if I'd seen the priest. I said, "Yes," and he said, "Okay, we won't talk anymore about it." It was a long time before I drew a picture of anything after that.

Dr. Field brought me out of trance and commented that this certainly went a long way toward explaining any creative block I might have.

"But even more than that," she went on. "Many issues are tied together here. The discouragement of creativity, the imposition of guilt feelings, the invasion of privacy, the forfeiture of parental responsibility…"

I suddenly got furious. "But I know all that!" I blurted out. "I've known it for years. I've got insight up the ass. But it hasn't made any difference. I'm more screwed up than ever!"

"Now, Shawn, that just isn't true."

"It is true! I've still got this Goddam idiotic weather hangup. I've lost my girlfriend. And if I don't get my act together soon, I'll lose my job."

"Now just a minute. Let's be accurate here. First of all, you've made a lot of progress with your "weather hangup", as you call it. And breaking up with Susan is not a bad thing. She isn't right for you and you know it. And as far as being blocked is concerned, every artist who ever lived went through it at one time or another. What makes you think you should be immune to a temporary dry spell?"

"But it isn't temporary. I can NEVER move easily through anything I create, whether it's a cartoon story or a painting or a novel. It's always like pushing a boulder up a mountain with my nose. I always get hung up worrying that no one is going to like it, no matter what it is I do. And right now it's worse than it's ever been."

Dr. Field listened patiently to my petulant diatribe and then offered a suggestion.

"Perhaps your difficulties aren't all rooted in this life. Maybe they're hangovers from John Williams."

"I don't know..."

"Well, maybe we can find out. How about going back and testing the idea?"

I was not convinced that exploring all this John Williams stuff, as fascinating and mysterious as it was, was going to get me any closer to breaking through this bind I was in. But, what did I have to lose except my mental chains? I agreed to go back once more and look around.

Dr. Field, as she always did, gave me the relaxation suggestions, and once more had me imagine myself on a train going faster and faster into the past. As she ticked off the years, I began to hear the sound of the wheels moving over the rails and feel the rocking motion of the car. Then there I was, in a compartment. I looked out the window and could see the buildings of the city speeding by. I was shuffling some papers on my lap. I couldn't seem to get them in order.

"Damn it!" I cursed in frustration.

"Is this John?" asked Dr. Field.

"It is indeed. What a bloody mess!"

"What's wrong?"

"It's my music. I've got it all mixed up."

"Where are you?"

"On the train to London."

"What year is it?"

"1923. Damn!"

"You say you've got your music mixed up?"

"Yeah. My sheet music. I've got all my songs here. Oh, Christ! We're coming to my stop!"

I grabbed up my manuscripts into an untidy pile, then made a dash for the exit just as we pulled in. I jumped off the train and was fifty feet down the platform when I saw the word "Paddington" on a sign overhead.

"Jesus Christ!"

"What's wrong now?"

"I've got off at the wrong station! Bloody hell!"

I scrambled back aboard the train just as it started to pull out. I made my way back to my compartment and plopped down on the seat.

"Now how did I do a bonehead thing like that? I wanted Euston Station."

"Where are you going?" asked Dr. Field.

"To a music company. I've written all these songs and I want to get them published."

"I didn't know you wrote music as well as playing it."

"Oh, yeah. I started back when I was a tyke. People are always telling me to show my songs to a publisher, but I don't know, I never fancied myself a pro until recently."

"So what makes you feel differently now?"

"Well, there's all this silly rubbish they're playing today on gramophone records, isn't there? My stuff is ten times better than any of that. And then there's this new thing – the wireless. It's getting to be all the rage. They're going to want tons of music for... Oh, will you look at that?"

"What's wrong now?"

"I've got my brief case wedged down between the seat and the wall. Can't pull it free. Excuse me a minute. I have to get some-one to help me pull this bugger out of here."

I looked outside my compartment and called the porter. He was a very slight fellow and was able to get his arm down in there and pull the case out for me. I tipped him half a crown, which was pretty extravagant, but I couldn't get off the train again without my case. Half of all my songs were in there.

Then I was getting off the train again, this time at the right station. I had straightened out all the sheet music, which I had paid a pretty penny to have professionally transcribed, and had it tucked away neatly in my case. As I headed for the bus stop,

I was feeling pretty chipper until I looked up. Then my spirits sank.

"What's the matter, John?" Dr. Field asked.

"It looks like it's going to rain. Always brings me down a peg – reminds me of France during the war."

"But you're not in France now. The war is over. It's been over for years."

"I know. But... Oh, damn! Does anything ever go right?"

"Now what's wrong?"

"No buses! And no cabs! There's a transport strike on! Seems like everybody's walking off the job these days. Well, I'll have to get to the publisher's on foot."

"Is it far?"

"No, but, as I said, it looks like rain and I don't have a brolly. I'll just have to quick-step it."

I could feel the sprinkles coming down as I moved quickly down the street. People were opening their umbrellas and ducking for cover into doorways and under awnings. After what seemed a very long walk, during which I got pretty wet, I turned into a big gray stone office building. As I tried to brush off the wet from my coat I looked around the old lobby and started muttering angrily again.

"Now what?" asked Dr. Field.

"The damned lift is out of order. I'll have to use the stairs."

Luckily the offices were only one flight up. I climbed the creaky wooden steps and began to hear a piano playing and someone singing. I couldn't make it out, but it was a typically silly popular tune. Something with an American flavor, like *It Ain't Gonna Rain No Mo*. The sounds of other pianos playing soon blended in, drowning each other out in a hodgepodge of dissonance.

Once I got to the landing, I could see great activity through the large glass windows that ran all along the wall. Lots of people, men in shirt sleeves at upright pianos and young women, rushing about while the music and singing got more and more cacophonous. I described this to Dr. Field as I moved along toward the far end of the floor to a door with a smoked glass panel on it. It had "Boles Booking, Ltd." lettered on the glass. I laughed.

"What's funny?" asked the doctor.

"The only thing I can't see through here is the entrance."

Because it said nothing on the door about music publishing I wondered if I were in the wrong place. I went inside. There was a young woman with very red lipstick and bobbed black hair seated at a reception desk. When I asked her if they published songs, she said, "Yes." But the company did more than that; it also booked talent for vaudeville. I told her my name and that I had an appointment to see Mr. Boles, and she told me to have a seat. Dr. Field asked me if there was anything special about my surroundings.

"It's a pretty tacky place. The carpet is very worn and dirty. Lots of cigarette butts everywhere. There's an older man with a trained dog sitting opposite me. The dog has a little conical hat perched on his head. The man is holding a big yellow scrapbook with hand lettered words on it. 'Winslow the Wonder Dog', it says."

After a few minutes, the young woman with the short hair called me over to her desk and told me that Mr. Boles had to step out and wouldn't be back until much later in the day and did I want to reschedule? I got quite angry.

"No, I don't want to reschedule. I've traveled a long way in and I want to see him today! I have some first rate tunes here and…"

She interrupted me and repeated that she didn't think he'd be back until much later, and it might be better to come another time.

"I'll go have a bite of lunch. Then I'll be back. Damn!" I grumbled and stomped out of the office.

Naturally, what I really wanted was not food, but a good stiff drink. It was raining quite steadily now. I spotted a pub just across the road and dashed over through the traffic. A truck driver blew his horn at me as I narrowly dodged out of his path.

"Up yours, you bloody twit!" I cried out.

"What's that all about?" asked Dr. Field.

"Lorry drivers! They let anybody drive these days!"

Once inside the pub I ordered a double whiskey and downed it quickly. Then I had another. Usually, a belt or two would mellow me out, but I was so angry at having come all the way into town and being brushed off that I just couldn't seem to cool down.

I struck up a conversation with a pretty young woman in a feathered hat sitting nearby. I mentioned that I'd just been in to see Boles.

"And he put you off." she said.

"Yes. How did you know?"

She told me she and her partner (She was half of a dance act) had had many encounters with Boles and he was notorious for not keeping appointments. This bit of news naturally called for another drink.

I don't know how many I had, but by the time I left the bar and went back up to see Mr. Boles I was seething. I ran up the stairs, barged into the office and demanded to see "His excellency". Once more the young lady receptionist told me he was out. But I was having none of it. I pushed past her and threw open the door back of her. There in a large, very messy office, sitting behind a big desk was a little bald man with a big cigar whom I took for Mr. Boles.

"What the hell do you want?" he asked.

I was so drunk, I'd forgotten what I'd come to see him about. I just ranted about being put off, pounding his desk with my fist and cursing a blue streak. The next thing I knew, I was being wrestled out of the office by two or three men. Nothing is very clear after that. I think I was either thrown or fell down the stairs. Then I was at the local police station. They sat me down on a bench and threatened to charge me with being drunk and disorderly if I didn't calm down. I must have been released later because the last thing I experienced was sitting on the wet curbstone, feeling sick and terribly ashamed. I think I even lost my case containing my music. But it didn't really matter because I knew I'd never again write a song or try to sell one. Dr. Field brought me out of trance at this point. We were right at the end of the hour and didn't have much time to discuss what had occurred, but she definitely saw a link between this event and my being creatively blocked. She thought it was a real revelation and a definite breakthrough. Having brought this event to the surface, she said she'd be surprised if I'd be staring at any more blank screens.

I left her office with my doubts. How would re-experiencing a stupid and painful event from an alleged other life help me to get rid of my writer's block? Like most of these visits to a past incarnation, it seemed pointless. But the closer I got to home, the itchier I was to get at my computer. I worked for a couple of hours that night, almost forgetting to eat any dinner. The next day I finished a first draft of my cartoon script, and also banged out several pages on the book I was doing. No, I didn't try to write any songs, but who knows what might have happened if I'd had a piano handy.

From the Therapist's Perspective

"Hell is full of musical amateurs."
—George Bernard Shaw, *Man and Superman*

*"Change happens when you slowly cross the bridge,
one small step, and then another."*
—Doctor Elly.

I was certainly impressed and delighted that Shawn had made so much progress on his own in moving forward toward recapturing the life and times of John Williams. Yet, from his point of view, he didn't seem to be able to make much progress in the life of Shawn Regan. Although he reported much less of a fearful reaction to the wind and the rain, he still maintained that the weather was bothering him. However, as I now watched him leave my office when it rained, he no longer looked frightened or lingered in the waiting room. He simply left and was on his way. He was also reporting walks and other activities in the rain. Why then did he seem to want to hang onto the idea that he was still uptight about the weather? There appeared to be a reason for his desire to hold onto the last strand of color in the rainbow.

It seemed like "stuck" pervaded his everyday life, stuck in the wind and stuck in the rain. And stuck on Susan. Why in heaven's name could he not get it through his noggin that she and he could never be a team? And he'd also been stuck from time zero with his creativity, or perhaps better said, without his creativity – "Can't write, can't get anything out". Like the kid in Freud's anal stage, he was showing Mama he just ain't gonna produce for her, not even on her pretty toilet seat.

Yes, I believed all this "constipation" was related. He needed to satisfy some need to be stuck. I suggested some age regression, not necessarily to his other life, but to wherever. And so Shawn went back to his mother's finding nude drawings and the ultimate punishment, his need to go to confession. Because of her own hang-ups as well as her religious beliefs and values,

Mom did indeed immobilize young Shawn. "If I draw or create, maybe it will be sexual, and that's bad and dirty. So better to block it. Right? Don't want my privacy invaded again. Don't want to feel more guilt feelings. They are too powerful."

For years, Shawn had these insights. But he could not put all of them into the right frame and glue them together. As we proceeded in our attempt to assemble a coherent picture, I suggested we check out his John Williams self as well. We did so, and indeed uncovered quite a situation. Now it was music, not words. Another disappointment, in fact, a total disaster. John *would never write another song*. And what else? It was raining again!

After the session, when Shawn arrived home that night, he wrote the songs that John could not, the songs of his present book and that first draft of his cartoon script. He did not need a piano to create these tunes. He was now performing "a cappella" – without accompaniment.

IX

The Cruise

IX

THE CRUISE

So I was once more turning out my work. I finished the book chapter, got it off in the mail, wrapped up the cartoon script and started on another project. I was on a roll. As I began sketching out a concept for a new cartoon series, I really felt great. I couldn't get the ideas down fast enough; that is, until it began to cloud up outside. Once more the old bugaboo started to crawl out of its hole. I closed the blinds and tried not to think about the possibility of showers and fixed my attention on my work, but that's what it was now, WORK. The ideas and gag situations suddenly evaporated.

I tried very hard to "tough it out", but something in the back of my mind elbowed its way forward. My thoughts were once more scanning across that terrible day when John Williams screwed up his chance to market his musical wares. But what came sharply into focus was not the fiasco in the booking office, and not even the fact that it had rained very hard that day and I'd gotten soaked, in more ways then one. No, what jumped out at me was the song I'd heard as I walked up that creaky old staircase – "It Ain't Gonna Rain No Mo'". Just a silly old novelty tune with inane lyrics. "How in the heck can I wash my neck if it ain't gonna rain no mo?". But the title seemed to grab hold of my mind. Maybe it would rain outside, but inside my head, "It ain't gonna rain no mo'!" Amazing how the unconscious mind communicates with the conscious mind. I was literally telling myself that I didn't need to feel frightened of the rain anymore. I looked again at the gathering clouds outside and for the first time in I couldn't remember when, I didn't feel intimidated. I still didn't like it, I still had some qualms, but I knew that even if it poured, I wasn't going to be kept from functioning. I went out my front door and looked furtively up and down the street to see if any of my neighbors were watching. Seeing none, I shot two middle fingers up at the clouds and made a rather rude noise with my mouth. Then I went back to my keyboard and began once more happily turning out the pages.

But nature was still playing its nasty games. We continued to have almost daily aftershocks from the big quake. They were all in the 3 to 4 range, enough to rattle your chain, but not enough to do serious damage. And after the cloudy weather passed, the hot Santana winds flared up. I don't think anybody had to go back to another life to find a reason to be disturbed by these occurrences. One of my neighbors called the combination of earth movements and hot winds "Mother Nature's menstrual pains". Even his dogs were acting freaky. But like everyone else in Los Angeles, I took another deep breath and pressed forward.

During the next couple of weeks I accelerated my work pace, trying to get everything out of the way before leaving on a Caribbean cruise – the one I'd repeatedly asked Susan to take with me. As busy as I was, Susan's face would still intrude on my thoughts occasionally. Then my brain would have a synapse lapse and I'd catch myself punching up her phone number, having totally blanked out the fact that she was in Japan. After I did that the third or fourth time, I wrote myself a sticky note and glued it on my telephone. It said: "She's GONE, you dumb son of a bitch!" She was gone alright, but certainly not forgotten.

Then three days before I flew to Puerto Rico, Susan called. She was back in town. I was surprised and delighted to hear her voice. We chatted about her trip and then I reminded her that I was leaving for the cruise. She wished me a good time, but when I asked her to have dinner with me once before I left, she became very frosty and abruptly turned me down. So, once more I was given the message – keep your distance. I was frankly pissed off, not at her but at yours truly for laying myself wide open to being cut off at the knees again. This was the first thing I brought up when I next saw Dr. Field.

"Well, what have I been telling you?" she said, a note of impatience in her voice.

"I know. See other women. Get her out of my system. Fine."

"So when are you going to get started?" she noodged.

"Soon. But please, don't bring up the dating service thing again, okay?" I said, feeling pressured.

"What about this cruise you're going to take? Maybe you'll meet someone on board."

It may be hard to believe, but the thought of connecting with the love of my life or even having a little shipboard fling seemed totally out of the question. And not just on account of my preoccupation with Susan. It was because, when it came to vacations and women, nothing ever went right. I sat silently for a moment, pondering all the chances I'd had over the years and how they'd gone sour. After a bit, Dr. Field broke in on my painful revery.

"What's happening, Shawn?"

"Huh? Oh, I'm just thinking about missed opportunities."

"You mean with the opposite sex?"

"Yeah. It seems like every time I go on vacation and I meet someone who's attractive and willing, I catch a cold or the flu or come down with diarrhea or some other dumb thing. I mean, every time!"

"Is this just when you go away?"

"Well it seems that way, but you know, when I think about it, it's happened other times, too. I remember when I first met Susan, we went out three or four times before we made love. But then that night, just as we were heading for the bedroom, I developed the God damndest backache you can imagine."

"And that stopped you?"

"Well, no. Susan was pretty determined. She got on top and did all the work."

Dr. Field prodded me to think of other examples. I thought back a few years to a time when I went through a period of unusual sexual activity.

"I just happened to meet three women almost simultaneously who were all hot to trot. It was great fun for a very brief time,
but I developed something that stopped me cold with all of
them."

"A venereal disease?"

"Well, no... Not exactly..."

"I don't understand."

"Well, I got this burning sensation when I'd urinate. But there
was no infection of any kind. The doctor called it 'non-specific
urethritis'. He said it was nothing contagious but that I ought to
knock off any sex until it went away."

Recalling this incident brought to mind several other times
when this same symptom had loused things up. I related a couple of those to Dr. Field as well. "Each time the doctor told me
the same thing – no infection, but lay off sex for a while and
you'll be okay. Hell, most of the time I hadn't even had any sex."

Dr. Field smiled. "Just what you wanted to hear, right?"

I laughed. "I'm sure."

"No, I mean it. Something in you WANTED to be told NOT to
enjoy any sex. Especially with three 'hot to trot' women."

"But why would I want to hear that?"

"Come on, Shawn. You've described getting nearly every psychosomatic ailment in the book. And it's always connected to
sex. What does that tell you?"

"That I have incredibly bad timing?"

"Now don't pass it off with a joke. What does that say to
you?"

"Okay. That I'm deliberately screwing myself – or maybe
UNscrewing myself. But why would I keep on doing that? Oh, I
know – all the Catholic guilt and my uptight mother and dirty
drawings, et cetera et cetera. But, my God, I'm hardly a kid anymore. You'd think that by now I'd have put all that behind me."

"Well, you obviously haven't."

"So what do I do? There's got to be a way to quit raining on
my own parade. Especially since the parade's almost gone by."

"Why don't we do some hypnosis? I can give you a post-hypnotic suggestion to help you avoid these pseudo-ailments while
you're on your trip."

"I'm for that. Let's go."

So Dr. Field had me in trance and spent the rest of the hour giving me suggestions about leaving my ills behind me. She had me visualize putting into a large steamer trunk every ache, pain, weather worry, etc. that could get in the way of my totally enjoying myself. Then, as the ship left the dock, she had me dump the trunk overboard.

A couple of days later I flew to Puerto Rico and boarded the ship. I was one of the last to get on, arriving at about 9:00 PM. I got my luggage to my cabin and ran up to the dining room where the second seating for dinner was already in progress. I spotted my friends Ted and Beth Forman from Wisconsin and had a very happy hugs and kisses reunion. However, there was no room at their table so I had to sit across the room. I introduced myself and everybody smiled and nodded, but then I realized nobody had understood me. Everyone at the table spoke nothing but German. Everyone, that is, except a very attractive woman sitting across from me. We had a hard time communicating because of all the Teutonic chattering, but I was able to find out her name, Megen, and that she was from New York.

After dinner we took a walk on deck and got acquainted. She worked in the fashion industry, at what I don't recall, but what impressed me most was her warmth and her sense of humor. She was very funny, telling me about some of the characters she worked with. But even more than that, she was sending out signals that she was definitely "interested". As we chatted, I started to have a few fantasies of finally "scoring" after all the years I'd been striking myself out. Megen invited me to have a drink with her. But she didn't have A drink. She had several – enough to get more stinko than Pepe le Pew. Drunk women are my second biggest turn on. My biggest is a hot poker up my nose. I finally got her unstuck from her barstool and steered her below to her cabin. All the way down she was on me like an old tattoo. Fortunately her cabin mate staggered along at the same time I got to her door. Dulcey, the other half of Alcoholics Unanimous, was equally blotto. While the two ladies decided to have their ninth nightcap, I slipped away faster than a gambler's paycheck. Despite this minor disappointment, the next couple of days were very enjoyable. Getting back with Ted and Beth was a big hoot. Ted knows more jokes than a standup comic and can tell them better than most. By the third day out I was really beginning to relax. But then, just as we were pulling into La Guerra, Venezuela, news came over the ship's satellite TV that Los Angeles had had another aftershock, only this time it was big – 5.3 on the Richter scale. That really sent a chill through me until I was able to call my neighbor who went over and inspected my house. Except for a few small items that had fallen off shelves, everything was apparently okay.

As for the elbow benders from New York, I'd see them every day, but I kept my distance. Megen was still sending out signals, but it was as though she were two different people – a pleasant, attractive woman by day and a falling down drunk at night. I wanted none of that. So, I figured, no romantic adventures this trip. So what if I wouldn't have a chance to test Dr. Field's post hypnotic suggestions? There would be other opportunities when I got home. Besides, I was with two delightful old friends.

But the next day we docked in Grenada and I met a really lovely young woman named Marisa. I spent most of the afternoon talking with her. She seemed much too young for me – she was thirty but looked twenty-one. Marisa was a Stanford graduate and an attorney. I was quite impressed by her, and she scored big with me when she showed a great deal of interest in my job of writing cartoons. When I said goodbye to her that afternoon, I thought what a lovely girl, but I won't see anymore of her. What would she want with an old geezer like me? Yet, that evening she sent drinks to everyone at our table.

And the next couple of days, when we docked in Barbados and then in St. Lucia, I ran into her in town both times. Even so, as friendly and warm and sexy as she was, because of our age disparity, I didn't even consider making any moves. But... when I again ran into her the next day in Martinique and she grabbed my arm as we walked through the streets, I got the message – this could happen. We made a kind of date for later in the evening.

As I dressed for dinner, my mind was full of schemes on how to get her down to my cabin. But right about then, I began to sense something going wrong inside me. I felt a cold coming on.

And even worse, that old burning sensation in my you-know-what came back. During dinner, I tried to talk myself out of my symptoms – maybe I had an allergy and maybe I'd had too much ice tea that afternoon, and maybe – Oh, who was I trying to kid? By the time they served dessert, I was coughing and sneezing and feeling like I had to pass battery acid.

So, when I did see Marisa later, I apologized and made it an early solitary evening. I was just getting out of my shirt and tie, cursing myself up and down for blowing yet another opportunity when there was a knock on my cabin door. It was Marisa. She had some antihistamine pills she thought would help me. I was so surprised that I could hardly speak. She told me to go right to bed and she'd see me in the morning. She gave me a little kiss on the cheek. She started to leave but then turned and asked, "You want me tuck you in?" I laughed nervously, like a junior high school kid. She gave me a devilish little grin and left.

Now I was really p.o.'ed at myself. I'd actually gotten her to my cabin and I still couldn't do anything about it. Several toilet articles ricocheted off the walls before I finally flopped into the sack. And, adding insult to impotence, I didn't notice the little chocolate mint the cabin steward had left on my bed. I woke up the next morning with some very unsightly and embarrassing streaks on my sheets.

The last two stops on our trip we docked at the very lovely islands of St. Maartin's and St. Thomas in the Virgin Islands. I saw more of Marisa, but never again were we alone together. I tried very hard to throw off my cold and my other "problem", but it was hopeless. Most of the time I was faking really hard having a good time. In St. Thomas, I bought a few gifts for friends back home and a very nice box of candy for Marisa. This got me a hug and another kiss and her phone number and address in Palo Alto. The next day I said my goodbyes to Marisa and to Ted and Beth. We boarded our planes and flew off to our homes. By the time I touched down in Los Angeles, my cold was all but gone as was my other difficulty.

Over the next few days, I thought many times of calling Marisa, but I had so many excuses for not doing so – our age difference, the long distance between our homes, etc.. I never saw or talked to her again. Why not? The truth was, I was so discouraged about the failure of Dr. Field's post-hypnotic suggestions that I didn't want to have anything to do with any women.

My first session with Dr. Field after the cruise was a stormy one. I made no secret of how disappointed I was, both in myself and in her therapy. As I blew off steam, she listened patiently. Once I got all my frustrations off my chest, the doctor made what proved to be a very important observation.

"Maybe the root of your problem goes much deeper. There might be something in John Williams' life that's responsible for perpetuating these self-defeating ailments. Why don't we go back and investigate?"

I was getting really tired of Mr. Williams. I wanted to write him a "Dear John" letter and put some space between myself and this dour drunken alter-ego from another time and place. But again I was getting drawn back to him and his era for a possible solution to a present day hangup. It was like exploratory surgery without anesthetic, but if there were any possibility of eliminating a lifetime of self-sabotage, I had to go for it.

As Dr. Field's trance induction took effect, I drifted back to a very inert, floating, dark, fluid existence. It seemed like I was not human. Maybe a fetus. I stayed in this state for several minutes before slipping back farther. Then I opened my eyes. All I could see was a blur of light. My eyes gradually focused in on the ceiling fixture with its one lit bulb. Then I saw the outline of a woman leaning over me.

"Is that you, John?" asked Dr. Field.

"Ooh... Yes..."

"What's happening?"

"I'm with a woman."

"Who is the woman with you? Is it Molly?" asked the doctor.

"I don't know. I don't recognize her."

"Do you know what year it is?"

"It's 1926."

I then got a better impression of the woman. Dr. Field asked me to describe her.

"She's a prostitute. Not terribly attractive. Might be in her thirties but looks older. She has "Mary Pickford" curls, trying to look younger than she is. She's got something purple or violet in her hair – it's an ornament of some sort. She's wearing an Oriental robe with a dragon design on it. Her teeth are very bad. Oh, Jesus!"

"What's wrong?"

"She's unbuttoning my knickers. She's telling me to relax – Oh, God! She's giving me oral sex! It's hurting me. I'm losing my erection. She's trying to get me to relax. Now she's pouring me a drink. I gulp it down. Oh, I feel like I'm going to be sick. The room is spinning."

Everything blanked out for a minute. Then I felt something wet on my face.

"What's happening now, John?" asked Dr. Field.

"The woman's wiping my face with a wet sponge. I'm sprawled out on the floor. I feel really awful – sick to my stomach with a very bad headache."

I started moving my head from side to side and groaning. The sponge smelled musty. I was lying next to an old fashioned bed with an ornamental metal headboard. The Oriental rug on the floor was very dirty. I could see a chamber pot underneath. The woman propped my head up. I felt the roughness of her hands on my neck.

"Feeling better now, Love?" the prostitute asked.

"What happened?"

"You were a little Tom and Dick." she said.

"What?"

"Sick. You brought up all over me."

"I did? I'm... sorry."

"Then you passed out and rolled off the bed. Is your head alright, Ducky? You had a nasty crack when you hit the floor."

My temples were throbbing as I pulled myself up onto the side of the disheveled bed. It was awkward, because my pants were down around my knees. I sat there for a moment, holding my head in my hands, not even bothering to button up. After a long pause, Dr. Field again asked me what was going on.

"I don't know. And, I don't remember how I met this woman or how I got here. I feel really dreadful."

The woman sat down next to me on the bed. She pulled up my pants and began to fasten the buttons on my fly. "I hate to do this to you, Love," she said, "but you have to go. I've got someone coming in a few minutes."

"Yes, of course," I said.

I staggered to my feet. I was still pretty woozy. She handed me my coat and hat, then she put her arm around me and helped me to the door. Just as she opened it I reached into my pocket to give her some money.

"That's alright, Love," she said. You already paid me. Now off you go."

I started to leave, but then I realized I didn't know where I was. She gave me a few directions and I left.

I soon found myself walking through a seedy section of London. It was late at night, but there were still a lot of people on the street. I seemed to know the area – it was a "red light" district and there were ladies of ill repute in every doorway. I pulled up my collar and pulled down my hat, hoping that I wouldn't run into anyone who would recognize me.

I described to Dr. Field how I walked and walked, and the more I walked the more my head cleared. I dimly recalled having gone earlier to a pub. I believe it was called, "Staley's". It was not my usual hangout. There were lots of easy ladies who frequented Staley's.

"Do you go there often?" asked Dr. Field.

"No. Hardly ever. But I had a fight with Molly and I didn't want to go home. God, I feel so ashamed."

"You mean for going to a prostitute?"

"Yes. And for cheating on Molly."

The night then seemed to fade away. For a moment I was once again in that fluid, inert state. Then it was daylight.

"Where are you now, John?" asked Dr. Field.

"In my shop."

"Is it still night?"

"No. It's a few days later. Ooh!"

"What's the matter?"

"Oh, I... I'm embarrassed to say."

"It's alright. You can tell me."

"Well, it's this burning sensation I get when I go to the loo. I believe I caught something from that woman."

"You mean a venereal disease?"

"Yes! Ow! Bloody hell!"

I squirmed in extreme discomfort. Then time moved quickly forward.

"Where are you now, John?" asked Dr. Field.

"In my doctor's office. I've been seeing him for several weeks. He's been treating me for venereal disease. It's been bloody awful."

"What kind of treatment?"

"He gives me sulphur injections. The most bloody painful things you can imagine."

The doctor entered the room. He was a tall, thin, balding man in his fifties or sixties with a very stern expression. Dr. Tennyson I believe was his name.

"What's the doctor doing?" asked Dr. Field.

"He's reading something from a file folder. Now he's examining my privates."

Dr. Tennyson told me I was through with the treatments, but I'd have to come back weekly to be checked out to see that the infection didn't return. Meantime, no sex. Then I began to squirm uneasily as he gave me a lecture about staying away from "loose women." Dr. Field picked up on my body language and asked me what I was feeling.

"Bloody embarrassed. And spilling over with guilt. I feel like I never want to go near any woman ever again."

Dr. Field had me focus in on what those feelings really "felt like" for me — the physical sensations in my body and where I felt them the most. She had me stay with those feelings for a very long time and until I experienced a release from those sensations. At this point she brought me back to the present, but requested I remain in a trance state. She was very excited about the connection we'd uncovered between John Williams' bitter experience and my present day compulsion to block myself off with psychosomatic ailments.

"And now we want to break that connection, once and for all," she said. She gave me the suggestion that from now on, freed from that situation and the inherent feelings, I would also be free to enjoy my sexuality unencumbered by any self-imposed pseudo-maladies. She then brought me back to full consciousness, although it took several minutes. (It always puzzled me why sometimes I could just pop back from a trance while other times it was so difficult.)

"We've done some very valuable work here today, Shawn," Dr. Field said.

Valuable indeed. To this date I've never had a recurrence of the kinds of ills I've described here. But...

From the Therapist's Perspective

"I am not afraid of storms,
for I am learning how to sail my ship."
—Louisa May Alcott

"The way I see it, if you want the rainbow,
you gotta put up with the rain."
—Dolly Parton

When a post-hypnotic suggestion, or any hypnotic suggestion for that matter, doesn't work, it's because you can't make something happen, not even with hypnosis — when there's something more underneath.

"Bloody embarrassed," says John, "and spilling over with guilt. I feel like I never want to go near a woman again."

Well, there's one way to accomplish that – have the physical symptoms to begin with, and that takes care of it all. Self imposed pseudo-maladies mean *no sex*. And, no sex means no possibility of contracting a venereal disease. Let's chalk off women completely and there's no chance of disease, embarrassment, guilt, those awful Dr. Tennyson treatments, and even those terrible "exploratory surgery" encounters "without anesthetic," per Dr. Field. In fact, let's cross out the Susan situation while we are at it, and we remove pain in the groin of another nature.

Earth-rattling excluded, as the aftershocks were affecting many people, Shawn's environmental problems seemed to be coming to a halt. In essence, Shawn still thought about the rain, as he describes, but the rain was no longer interfering with his functioning. The song, "It Ain't Gonna Rain No Mo," had really taken hold of his mind. Amazing how that song filtered down from the John situation, like so much else had. Shawn's relating this to me only caused me to believe that other aspects of his behavior might find their roots back there with John as well.

As for Shawn's still "noticing" the rain, it was to be expected. It's like a smoker's freeing himself from nicotine. He stops the habit of taking a cigarette, but it takes a longer time before he *remembers to forget* about wanting one, or *forgets to remember* about them. After time has passed, where he has successfully *remembered to remember* that he is now "free", his thought processes turn elsewhere and he completely *forgets about smoking*.

I was delighted to hear that Shawn had accomplished so much of his work prior to leaving on his cruise. But Susan remained a bone of contention. He wasn't about to give her up without a big internal fight. It was obvious she was out of his life, but Shawn needed time in order to accept this. It's like mourning a person who has died. First comes *denial*, and then, finally, with time and struggle, comes the reality of the *acceptance* that that person is gone forever.*

Since Shawn had on several occasions asked my opinion of that relationship, I was completely direct with him. At this point, I encouraged his accepting the reality of the situation. But I wondered if he still had to go through more of the other phases of the process, such as continuing to *bargain* with himself... "Maybe if I call her she'll have dinner with me before I leave on the cruise." He finally showed the usual symptoms of *depression* which come about when all is realized as lost. It was then that I encouraged him to "let go" and to seek other women. I believe in **action** and so as Shawn puts it, I "noodged".

The cruise might have provided such an opportunity for Shawn, but then came the pseudo-maladies self-sabotage. When he returned home from his Caribbean adventure, and reported the happenings "as usual", I gave him all the space he needed to rant and rave about his disappointments. Then I had him forget all the thoughts in his head and focus in on those sad and angry feelings at a body-sensation level. "Forget the thoughts and really feel the sensations of what those feelings feel like for you; the

---

* The steps which make up the process of mourning per Elizabeth Kubler-Ross:
    D - Denial
    A - Anger
    B - Bargaining
    D - Depression
    A - Acceptance

tightness, the strain (anger is felt in the gut), perhaps the inability to swallow what had occurred (sadness is usually felt in the throat, often manifesting the inability to swallow, from which is derived the metaphor, 'I can't swallow it.').'' Experiencing feelings, or the "Feeling Focus" process, is the essence of release. I believe this to be most important before moving on.

Indeed, we found what we were looking for in the John Williams escapade, an escapade which resulted in the identical burning sensations which Shawn had experienced on the cruise. My sense was there were many issues interwoven here. Shawn had expressed sadness, pain, and loss. He certainly lost on that cruise by way of his cold symptoms, his burning sensations in his groin, and whatever other psychosomatic symptoms had plagued him. Pain indeed! It was astonishing how he appeared to be even carrying with him John's final "gift" from that prostitute.

Yes, there seemed to be many apparent connections to John Williams and his misadventures. John had lost firstly his parents, then his Maggie, and then he could have been concerned about possibly losing Molly's love, a loss which he was helping to create. He chose the company of a prostitute, probably to express his fear of marriage and fear of Molly's love, by way of indulging in infidelity. He also accomplished this by fighting with Molly and not wanting to return home. Had John kept his "Fear of Abandonment Script" going by way of working hard to cause it to occur? If he screwed around enough, certainly Molly would leave him. That guy didn't know when to quit and when to accept the love he was offered. He was just not accustomed to accepting being loved and cared for. He, for sure, feared being left again.

So what about Shawn? Yes; he lost Susan as he had lost other ladies. Now he feared *change*. *Change* is something unknown. What losses could *change* carry with Her Sultry Mysterious Self?

Shawn had lost in love and more than once. He also lost every time he feared completing whatever he was working on, a fear he had expressed many times. Could his difficulty in finishing be related to his difficulty in finishing sex? Or could it be the other way around? In other words, was his difficulty in finishing sex in keeping with his inability to reach the finish line in other areas? At one point, the prostitute says to John, "You have to leave, Love." She had "somebody else coming in a few minutes". So John was sent away, one more strike on the abandonment match. If John couldn't "come", he could "go", just as Susan told Shawn to go, but of course, not in those words.

Now, all had come full circle. Some very significant ties were incredibly apparent. And now those ties had to be untied. When answers are found, the last rung on the regression therapy ladder is to sever the ties to that which bridges the past to the present. Thus, I gave Shawn the following suggestions:

"Now that you are aware of what occurred with John, knowing that you are not John, that he is from another life, and that you are now Shawn— not John, and you have no reason to carry his guilt as a part of you today— knowing you are *YOU*— would it be alright to give up that burden, let go of it, and function freely? Would it be alright to be free from all of that past and now be able to experience and enjoy, among other things, your sexuality and your ability to fully relate to members of the opposite sex, from this time forward and forevermore?"

When I received a "Yes" from Shawn's index or "Yes" finger, I then had him imagine his writing the date on a chalkboard as to when he would let go and be over all we had explored...and be free and functioning. Shawn replied with the date of *THAT DAY*, the day of that very important and valuable session. And to *THIS DAY*, Shawn has indeed been free.

X

Setting The Stage

X

SETTING THE STAGE

*T*hese were very troubling days. Everywhere I looked, it seemed, there was bad news. My personal life stunk, the stock market was tumbling, the aftershocks kept coming, and for the first time in many years I felt that my job was in jeopardy. I still had an excellent relationship with my boss, but the company had undergone an unfriendly takeover by a corporate giant. A whole new administration came in and started cleaning house. Many of the most talented artists and writers in the industry, people who had been with the studio for years, were being let go. For the moment I had plenty of work to do, but there was no telling when the new management would be dropping the ax on me. Even though I'd only recently had a vacation, just being in Los Angeles made me so glum that I felt the need to once more leave town. On an impulse, I decided to fly up to Washington to visit my brother. This trip would be different from the usual get together, however, because I decided to look for a place to move. I actually made an offer on a condo, but I withdrew a few days later. I was so sick of earthquakes and all the other L.A. blues, that I forgot how much it rained in the Northwest. And although I was not as bothered by precipitation as before, it was still a problem. So I returned to Southern California, feeling like yesterday's pancakes. But the fire under my griddle was turned up a notch when I saw Dr. Field late in the afternoon. I reviewed with her what had been happening since our last meeting.

"I feel like I have nothing I can hang onto. Not my job, not my girlfriend, not even the ground I walk on. It's like everybody and everything is just letting me go. I really feel like I've been blown out of the water and cast adrift."

"Does this feeling of being 'let go' remind you of anything we've dealt with before?"

"Of course. It's the whole theme of John Williams' life, isn't it? Or should I say, wasn't it?"

"Yes. But it's not really the theme of YOUR life, is it? You and I have talked at great length about your background and the traumatic events of your life. And while you've certainly had some tough times, you, Shawn, haven't had the kinds of experiences that would warrant such a terrible fear of abandonment. Your parents did not leave you. You never had a wife leave you. You've broken up with girlfriends with the usual amount of anxiety, but you've gone on to others. And you've had jobs you left, only to land even better ones. So putting your present situation in such dramatic terms as being 'blown out of the water' and 'cast adrift' doesn't quite fit you. But it does fit John Williams."

I went silent for a few moments. I had a lot to digest here and much of it was sticking in my throat. I was still on the fence about reincarnation, leaning over backwards toward any other explanation of all these visitations into a supposed other life. But what Dr. Field had brought up was quite valid. Why would I feel so much like a lost soul because of the setbacks I'd recently had? I was a big boy. I'd handled much rougher situations, like taking care of two sick and dying parents, and I'd come through without feeling totally lost. And even going back to my rain and wind terror, which I'd never had until recent times – where did that come from? We'd tried for months to nail it down, searching around in Shawn Regan's past, but without success. It wasn't until John Williams made his surprise appearance that feeling this terrible fear made any sense... AND started to abate. Where did all that anxiety come from, if not from another existence?

I guess my facial expressions revealed all the machinations my mind was going through because Dr. Field began to chuckle.

"What's going on in there?" she asked.

"You really got my wheels turning with that one, Doctor," I finally conceded. "You realize what you're saying – that my present feelings are really from another person?"

"Shawn, this is all uncharted territory to both of us. All I'm suggesting is that the shoe fits somebody else better than it fits you. Whether John Williams was an actual person who lived at another time or whether he's a hidden part of your own being, the only way we've gotten any results alleviating your suffering has been to deal with him directly."

"Then you think that if we went back and visited old J.W. again, maybe we could get to the bottom of this separation panic I've had lately?"

"I certainly think it's worth doing."

So once again I agreed to let Dr. Field take me back to the life and times of John Williams. As usual, she eased me into trance with a series of calming suggestions. Then she guided me back to the year 1928.

"Are you there, John?"

I didn't answer right away. I felt like I was being awakened from a deep sleep. I had a headache which seemed to grow more intense as I opened my eyes. I also felt very queasy. It was a familiar set of symptoms. I was hung over.

"John?" she again asked.

"Yeah, yeah."

I rubbed my head and frowned as my dry tongue tried to find a moist spot in my sandpaper mouth.

"Where are you, John?"

"Where the bloody hell do you think I am? You can see for yourself I'm in the kip. Oh, God I've got a head!"

"Were you out drinking last night?"

"Saturday night? Well, I hope to tell you. I'd hate to think I feel this bad for nothing."

I looked around the bedroom. It was far too clean and tidy to be mine. I recognized I was in my lady friend's flat.

"Maggie!" I called out. "Maggie! Have you got the kettle on?"

She entered the room wearing a blue dress trimmed in black. She had on a small black hat and was carrying a tray with a tea pot and two cups on it. She looked very angry. "Damn you!" she grumbled between clenched teeth.

"What's wrong?"

"My name is MOLLY, not Maggie."

She slammed the tray down on the side table, almost spilling the tea.

"What? Oh. Did I do that again?"

"What's it been – ten years since you've seen the woman? And you're still getting our names mixed up."

"I... I'm sorry," I muttered sheepishly.

"I don't know why I put up with you." She poured tea into a cup and gave it to me. My hands shook as I brought it to my lips. "You keep that woman between us like a wall. I can't understand for the life of me why you don't divorce her so we can be married."

"You know why. I've told you over and over. I'm Catholic. Catholics don't get divorced."

"Well then, if you're such a God-fearing man, get your holy backside out of that bed and come to church with me this morning."

"Why do we have to go through this routine every Sunday morning of our lives? I'm a Catholic. Not a bloody Anglican. I don't go to the Church of England."

"You don't go to any church. You haven't seen the inside of one since you came back from the war."

"Doesn't matter. I'm still a Catholic."

Molly shrugged, swallowed her tea and stood up. "Well, I'm off. There's bread and jam on the sideboard and the headache powders are in the cabinet. Oh, and one more thing..." She picked up her purse and pulled out her lipstick. Then she wrote her name with it across the mirror over the dresser. "... Just in case you forget... Again!" She left the room and slammed the outer door.

I'd been relating all this to Dr. Field but now, with Molly gone to church, I pulled a pillow over my head and tried to go back to sleep. I was silent for quite a while, but Dr. Field picked up on my body language.

"You seem to be tossing and turning, John," she said.

"I am. I feel ruddy awful."

"Your hangover?"

"Not just that. I feel terribly guilty."

"About what?"

"Oh, the whole business here with Mag – I mean, Molly. She's so good to me and I just keep stringing her along. I wouldn't blame her in the least if she up and left me."

"But to have someone abandon you – again – that would be just about the worst thing that could happen, wouldn't it?"

"Yes. I don't think I could tolerate it."

"Well, what are you going to do – "

"Please! I don't want to talk about this anymore."

Dr. Field backed off for the moment. But she didn't bring me out of trance. It seemed like I fell asleep, but then after a minute or two I was awake again and dressed, moving about Molly's kitchen. I was looking through drawers.

"Damn, where is it?" I muttered.

"Where is what, John?" Dr. Field inquired.

"The bread knife. I want to make myself some toast, but I can't find the ruddy bread knife."

At this point, the door opened and Molly returned from church. She had a big paper sack and its contents smelled very fragrant.

"What's that?" I asked.

"Some breakfast rolls and cakes," she said.

"From the Jewish bakery?"

"I know how much you like them."

She made some more tea and we sat down to eat, not saying much to each other. Then Molly went to the cupboard and brought out a cigar box. She took out the last cigar. She slid off the band, put the cigar in my mouth and lit it. This was a little ritual we went through every Sunday morning after breakfast. I don't know how it got started, but that's what she always did. I usually smoked cigarettes, so it was something special. As I sat there puffing away, Molly reached across the table and took my hand.

"I'm sorry about that little episode in the bedroom this morning," she said. "It wasn't exactly the nicest thing to do just before church."

Then I did something very odd. Without thinking, I picked up the cigar band and put it on Molly's middle finger. She looked surprised. Then she looked angry.

"What's this, then?" she said.

"It's an I Love You Ring," I said, jokingly. But she wasn't having any of it.

"I Love You Ring! Indeed!"

"But – "

"You know what kind of ring I want and it doesn't come wrapped around a cigar!"

"But I only meant to – "

"I think you'd better go home, Mister Williams." Molly was close to tears.

"Look, I'm sorry I've upset you. What can I do to make it up?"

"You can kill Maggie!" she shouted. She was crying now.

"Kill Maggie? Are you balmy?"

Molly picked up the cigar box and went to a linen cupboard. She reached behind some towels and pulled out an old pin cushion doll. She stuffed it in the box and shoved it at me.

"There. There's your Maggie. Take her out and bury her!" She pushed the cigar box into my hands. I'd never seen her so livid. "Go on! Dig a hole and bury her deep! And don't come back here 'till you do!"

She pushed me toward the door. Then everything went blank.

Dr. Field waited a few moments, hoping that more information would emerge, but I just sat there and shuddered. She decided then to bring me out of trance. We were way past our usual time to stop, so we talked only briefly about this very surprising and upsetting turn of events. We'd have to wait until our next session to bring this burial business into some kind of perspective.

Although it was very unpleasant, to say the least, my John Williams encounter with Molly had put a charge into me. All the way home, I felt a great sense of exhilaration. I'd gone from cold flapjacks to hot cross buns. What exactly I was so excited about I wasn't sure, but I knew we'd touched on something really important. It wasn't until I turned into my driveway that I realized I'd driven all the way home through some pretty heavy rain. I'd been so distracted that I'd forgotten to be scared.

My birthday was fast approaching. I was again busy with a script, but as each day passed, I found myself jumping out of my chair every few minutes, looking for the mailman. I got several cards, including two from former girl friends. I was even taken out to lunch by one of them. There was no attempt to rekindle old sparks, just friendly conversation. I was quite pleased that so many people remembered my natal number, including Dr. Field, who presented me with a surprise birthday cake at our next session. But as happy as I was to be in people's thoughts, I was disappointed that I didn't hear from Susan. I knew I had no right to expect anything from her anymore, and yet there was still something in me that wanted something of her, even if it were just a second-hand sentiment by Hallmark.

Dr. Field seized on this lingering longing for Susan.

"In your mind, Shawn, Susan serves the same function that Maggie does for John – they're both protective barriers to a meaningful relationship. So as long as John is hung up on Maggie, Shawn is hung up on Susan."

"But, if that's true, I'm screwed."

"What do you mean?"

"Well, from all we've been able to bring up from the past, John never really got over Maggie."

"We don't know that for sure. But even if he didn't, our last session gave us a possible method for severing that connection."

"You mean that doll-in-the-cigar-box business?"

"Yes."

"So, you think I should go out and get a cigar box and – "

"No, no. Not you. John needs to do that. I think we should go back and see if we can get John to do it."

"Is that possible? All I've ever done is re-experience what supposedly happened in the past. Wouldn't this be like rewriting history?"

"You could look at it that way. But remember what we're trying to do here. We're attempting to free you from your obsession with Susan. Isn't that worth a little revisionism?"

"I suppose so." I began to laugh.

"What's funny?"

"I was just thinking what this conversation would sound like to someone listening at the door. Here we sit, trying to get some dude in a past life to bury a doll in a cigar box so I can break it off with my girl friend – anybody who heard that would undoubtedly want to have us both locked up."

"Believe me, Shawn, there have been lots crazier things than that said in this room. That's why it has a double thick door. Now let's begin, okay?"

So we once more set forth on a journey back to John Williams and his era. Dr. Field used the usual method – lots of relaxation suggestions, followed by another train trip back through time. Then my vision went dark for a brief period, during which I began to sense a strong but very agreeable odor. It was the smell of finished leather. As my vision became brighter and less blurred, I looked around and discovered myself, as John, in my shoe shop. I was in the back room, my work room, where I was putting the finishing touches on a very smart looking pair of men's riding boots. I related this to Dr. Field and the fact that I was having a hard time keeping my mind on my work.

"Why is that, John?" she asked.

"Because of Molly."

"What about her?"

"I haven't seen her in several days."

"Did she go away?"

"No. She sent me away. Said she didn't want to see me anymore."

"Has this happened before?"

"Yeah, but we always made up before this many days'd gone by. She doesn't even want me to come into the pub where she works. I tell you it's eating me up inside." I opened a drawer and pulled out a pint bottle of whiskey. I poured a stiff one into a glass and drank it down in one swallow.

"Does it have anything to do with your drinking?"

"Not really. She's all in a stew about the usual things – marriage and Maggie."

"John, whatever happened to that cigar box with the pin cushion doll that Molly gave you?"

"Oh, I don't know. I put it away someplace."

"Isn't this it here – at the end of your work bench?"

"What? Oh, yes."

Now here is a tricky thing to explain. As John, I now saw the cigar box, and yet Shawn knew it wasn't real. It was as if the Shawn part of me was sitting on the sidelines taking in this whole scene. It was truly like being two people at once.

Dr. Field continued: "John, do you know why Molly wanted you to bury this cigar box with the doll in it?"

"Oh, it was some silly voodoo kind of thing – "

"Wasn't it because she wanted you to put Maggie out of your life, once and for all?"

"Yeah. That was what she wanted."

"Do you want that?"

"Certainly. But I don't see how burying something in the garden is going to make a farthing's worth of difference."

"Would you do it just to please Molly?"

"But it's so absurd."

"But what if burying the cigar box would bring Molly back to you?"

"... Well... Oh, alright."

As John, I picked up the cigar box and went out the back door to a small garden area. At first it was confusing, because it was not my garden. It was Molly's garden. Then she was there, by my side. She was holding a small shovel. Without speaking, she handed it to me. I dug a shallow hole, dropped the box into it, then covered it over with dirt.

"There," I said, as I patted the dirt down. "I suppose I should sing a hymn now."

Molly took my hand.

"Do you feel any differently?" asked Dr. Field.

I suddenly had a catch in my throat. I couldn't speak for a long moment. I felt very sad.

"John? What's happening?" asked Dr. Field.

"Please," I said, choking back tears. "Leave me alone. Just leave me alone." I dropped the shovel, let go of Molly's hand and walked away, back into my shop. I closed the door behind me.

Then I was Shawn again. I'd been observing all this from a detached point of view. Now I too felt John's sadness. But I also felt my own sense of great relief.

From the Therapist's Perspective

"Love is a fruit in season at all times
and within reach of every hand."
—Mother Theresa

"Whoever lives true life
will love true love"
—Elizabeth Barrett Browning

Cleaning house! Shawn begins this chapter talking about his studio's being in the process of doing just that. Realistically, he knew that his job was in jeopardy, but meanwhile, he was still in their employ. While he felt "swept away" by others having cleaned house with him, Shawn was really not under the broom, with the exception of the Susan-Let-Go situation. Yet, he was feeling "blown out of the water".

I sensed it was time for Shawn to start separating from the John experiences. Indeed, the John revelations had explained so much. Perhaps, now it was time to psychically clean house and break away from John. I did not mean for Shawn to forget John or all John's impact upon Shawn's present day self. I meant that Shawn needed to separate and individuate himself. He needed to slice the two apart. Shawn was Shawn. Shawn was not John. With all the important material he had learned from John, Shawn needed to realize that he was HE today, and HE needed to let go of continuing to impose that old stuff upon his life. This is not at all different from the patient who recaps material from an earlier point in his life, perhaps from his childhood, which explains his behavior today. Upon recalling this, and working through the feelings therein, that person finally realizes he no longer has to please his mother, nor does he need to listen to his father's verbal abuse, nor take on any guilt from that era. He is now grown up and living his own adult life. The only one he needs to please today is himself. When I presented these thoughts to Shawn, they appeared to have considerable impact. He had to digest them slowly. That was OK. I was impressed with the time he spent assimilating the concepts I had presented that day. I knew they were permeating his psyche.

It was also interesting that this followed his visit with his boss, who came over so positively. I had the feeling that more doors were going to open real soon for Shawn. Separation stuff, indeed. Shawn was to become the custodian and the cleaner rather than the one to be cleaned or "cast adrift".

What occurs now is interesting because I had, on an occasion when Shawn was in a trance state, talked about John's "burying" Maggie. Now Molly sets the stage for John's doing that. In fact, I had previously asked Shawn to think about how John could accomplish this. Was this the end result of that suggestion I had given to John's subconscious earlier, or did it simply occur on its own? It really didn't matter. The fact was that it was happening! And that was gratifying.

As an end result of Molly's challenge to bury Maggie, Shawn felt energized. I conjectured that the impact of John's marriage to Maggie, although it had only lasted one year, that union had had a really deep effect on Shawn today.

As Shawn related, so many people remembered his birthday this year. Although this is not in the usual realm of therapy, I personally enjoyed ordering him an Irish Green frosted birthday cake decorated with "Happy Birthday to Shawn and John". There seemed to be a special ring to this particular birthday. Yet, Shawn still longed for a little something from his Susan. Susan to Shawn was like Maggie to John, an unavailable entity which kept the other from moving forward.

And so John digs a hole in Molly's garden and drops into it the little cigar box with the pin cushion doll. Together, they attend the funeral and burial.

It is remarkable how meaningful and therapeutic psychologists have found such little acts to be. You can never rewrite the life script but *you can write over it*. The end result produces a different twist to the patient's life. Up to this point, from that hypnosis session, Shawn reports, "It was truly like being two people at once." Now he reports, "I too felt John's sadness. But I also felt my own sense of relief."

As John walked back into his shop and closed the door, I believe Shawn also closed the door on his attachment to that wife of another life. Somehow, I believe that Maggie had an impact on Shawn's intimate relationships in this life. All of his relationships to that point had turned to dust. Like John's marriage to Maggie, they had all disintegrated. Could Susan of this life be a representation of John's Maggie from the other life? Perhaps, Susan couldn't take the waiting for Shawn to free himself from his fears, just like Maggie "couldn't take the waitin'" for John to come home from the war. Had Shawn, by way of his subconscious mind, chosen women who would in some way, like Maggie, ultimately leave him, women who were not really compatible?

Now that John had buried Maggie and Shawn had sufficiently severed his ties with John...Shawn was prepared to journey forward and select a new road upon which to travel. Shawn was now completely free, free and ready to accept intimacy and a genuine relationship in this life. But I did not verbalize this to him at the close of that session. I let him *BE*...to experience fully "the sadness"...and finally... "the relief".

XI

Severing The Ties

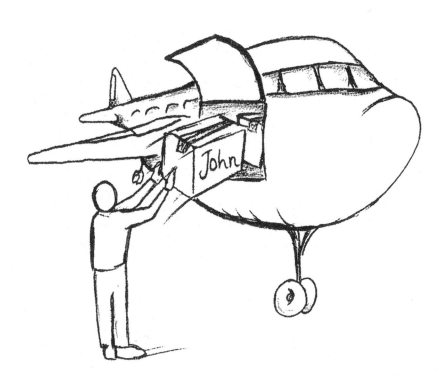

XI

SEVERING THE TIES

*Y*es, I felt a great relief. But whether the effects of that little ritual with the doll and the cigar box were permanent or temporary would only be demonstrated by the passage of time.

Meanwhile, I had many other things on my mind, all of which had to do with survival. As I mentioned earlier, there was a great shakeup going on at the studio. And even though I'd had many years of experience writing animated cartoons, there was no security in knowing my craft. As has happened in all phases of film and television in recent years, the idea that younger is better was now the de facto company policy. It was particularly disturbing to hear the new studio head boast that in his last job he refused to have anyone over thirty working for him.

So, I pushed myself into high gear. In addition to writing a pilot script for a new series, I was also developing projects of my own, including written presentations, a script and artwork. And, I was calling and having meetings with people I knew in the business, hoping to get myself lined up with another job before the new top brass decided to show me the door. I was running harder than a centipede on a treadmill. After about three weeks of this kind of hyperactivity, my body began sending me disturbing signals. I started having chest pains. And my heart was banging around inside me like a gorilla locked in a clothes closet. This prompted a visit to my doctor. No, I wasn't having a heart attack and this was not my old fibrillation problem, he said. Just a lot of anxiety and not enough sleep. Relax. Take 'er easy. Get some rest. Uh huh. Right.

I was scheduled to see Dr. Field the following day. I had hopes that she could help me lighten up and get rid of these symptoms which I assumed were caused by the workload I had imposed upon myself. She gave me a few relaxation suggestions, and they seemed to work, at least partially. My heart calmed down, but I still had the extreme discomfort in my chest. It was then that Dr. Field conjectured that the source of my suffering might not be overwork.

"If not, then what?" I asked.

In a classic shrink maneuver, Dr. Field turned the question around. "What do YOU think?"

"I don't know... Maybe..."

"Yes? Maybe what?"

"I don't want to keep going back to John Williams. But since the pain doesn't seem to be connected to what's going on with me here and now, maybe it has something to do with his life."

"Maybe it does," she replied. "You're shaking your head."

"Oh, it's just that every time I say something like that, you know, putting my problems on John that is, I feel like I'm copping out. Besides..."

"Yes?"

"Well, this thing in my chest is a lot like the stabbing sensation that got this whole past life business started. I thought we'd dealt with that and put it to rest."

"There's always the possibility of unfinished business. Do you want to go back and see if it clears it up?"

"I'm not sure I do. Frankly, I'm leery of dealing with a possible life threatening situation again. It's too damned scary."

"I understand. If we get into an area that's overly sensitive, I can always give you the suggestion that you're viewing it from a safe distance."

"Well, okay." I took a deep breath, preparing for the worst. Despite Dr. Field's assurances, I feared I was in for a bumpy ride, which is probably why she had a little more trouble than usual getting me to let loose enough to go under. Even as I drifted off into deep hypnosis, I was still apprehensive. She told me to wiggle a finger on my right hand should I get into trouble I felt I couldn't handle. Obviously, deep inside me I knew something very disagreeable was about to take place. Sure enough – there I was again, in that God damned trench, shells exploding all around me. Before I had a chance to give Dr. Field any kind of signal, the terrifying silhouette of that same German soldier appeared above me. He leapt at me with his bayonet, and I let out a scream that must have been heard all through the building. Dr. Field quickly told me it was okay, that what was happening was on a motion picture screen, and that I could view it without feeling threatened. Easy for her to say.

Suddenly I was riding along in the back of truck, feeling every lurching, jarring movement shoot through my torso. Again I cried out in agony. If this was like watching a movie, the special effects were overpowering. Again, I heard Dr. Field's voice, telling me I was in no danger, that I could step outside this experience and see it without any kind of threat. I felt then as though I were fading away – and for a moment I was quite calm. But now came the real jolt – instantly, I was Shawn, back in my own bedroom, re-experiencing the earthquake. Again, for an absolutely awful moment, I feared I was going to die. More screaming.

At this point, Dr. Field decided she'd better bring me out of trance. I was off on some kind of trip of my own and wasn't responding to her suggestions that I could view these events from a detached point of view. It didn't take her long to get me back, but even when I was once again in the "here and now", I was so shaken I began to sob. She just let me go on for a while, then asked, "What's happening, Shawn?"

The pain in my chest continued to be intense. "I don't know, exactly. It's just that all these things, the bayoneting, the earthquake and Susan all seem to come together."

"What's the connection?"

"It's like there's a war shaking me like crazy inside, and I've been stabbed twice. Once by that German soldier and once by…"

"By Susan?"

"Yes. When she cut me loose."

"Interesting choice of words – So she STABBED you and CUT you?"

"That's the feeling. But I know she never intended to hurt me. She had every right to break it off."

"So all's fair in love and war, eh?" said Dr. Field. I was too upset to appreciate the irony of her remark.

Once more I started to cry, overwhelmed by the many forces that seemed to be ganging up on me. "Everything that's important to me – the love of a woman, my security, my job, my very life – all these things feel like they're being smashed."

I felt like I was going to pieces, too. But Dr. Field began giving me suggestions to release all these dark thoughts and to relax. It took a while, but I did eventually calm down. Yet that awful stabbing pain in my chest persisted.

Dr. Field once more took me back to being John. Only this time she set the scene for me – a very safe, comfortable chair in my own home. She suggested that Molly appear. Then, doing a bit of role playing as Molly, she very lightly stroked my chest and began to soothe the hurt. Little by little it melted away. Then she brought me back to full consciousness.

"How do you feel now, Shawn?"

"Much better. But I'm pretty wrung out."

"I have to congratulate you for having the courage to deal with all these painful things."

"Thanks. But what's it gotten me?"

"Well, for one thing, you don't have the stabbing feeling anymore, right?"

I rubbed my chest and nodded.

"You hit yourself with the full weight of your own life's problems and John's. That took a lot of strength. But..."

"But what?"

"You don't want John's problems reinforcing your own. You have to separate out the two. The emotional overload is too draining."

"You can say that again. I've got enough to handle in my own life without dragging old John's baggage around with me."

"Exactly. So, let's go down the list. Tell me some problems John has that you don't."

"Well, he's a drunk. I don't drink at all."

"Okay – what else?"

"He was severely wounded in a war. I was never even in active service."

"Yes?"

"He was abandoned by his parents and his wife...wait a minute..."

"What?"

"As I was saying that, a couple of bells went off. First, it does seem like my parents abandoned me. And so did Susan."

"But that's not really true, is it?"

"Well, my parents both passed away within the last three years. Now that's not the exact same thing, but – "

"It certainly isn't. I know you miss them, but you must see that's a far cry from John's situation. After all, he was left in an orphanage at an early age. Your parents – "

"Okay. I see that. Right. But what about Susan? She dumped me just like Maggie dumped John."

"Again, John's situation was different in many ways."

"How so?"

Again, in that way that psychologists have, Dr. Field turned the tables and asked me to tell her the answer to my own question. I thought about it for a minute, then responded.

"... Well, I suppose the fact that John and Maggie were married."

"And you and Susan weren't. As a matter of fact, you weren't even living together. Right?"

"Right."

"Okay, what else?"

"Well, with John, he never heard from Maggie again. Susan and I still talk occasionally."

"Anything else?"

"I'm disappointed that our relationship didn't work, but I don't have the bitterness toward Susan that John had toward Maggie. John always felt that Maggie deliberately meant to hurt him. I never felt that with Susan."

"Good. Can you think of any other problem of John's that you don't have?"

"Well, John just couldn't seem to let go of Maggie and commit to Molly or any woman, and I... oop!"

"Oop?"

"I think John and I may be on the same page here."

"You may be. But I think you're at the bottom of that page."

"What does that mean?"

"It means that you're just about ready to turn to the next chapter and connect with someone permanently."

"You think so?"

"I do. And speaking of that..."

"Oh, no! You're not going to bring up the dating service thing again, are you?"

"Okay, we'll put that on the back burner for now. But I do think you're ready to say goodbye for good to Susan and to move on."

"I hope you're right. But how can you be sure?"

"Because of what happened a few moments ago. When Molly was able to relieve you of your pain, your 'heartache', if you will, I believe you literally got Susan 'off your chest'." At this point, Dr. Field's big grandfather clock started chiming the hour. It was a good moment on which to end the session because it gave me a lot to mull over and digest before we would next meet. Had I indeed ended my heartache and truly gotten Susan "off my chest"? And what about John – had ticking off all these differences helped me to cut the chord to his miserable life? I had high hopes, and being relieved of the chest pain, I felt a burst of new energy. That night, I went to the gym and swam a hundred laps in the pool. The next few days were again packed with activity, but this time without the physical and emotional symptoms I'd had previously. I continued to work on my pilot script and my own projects. And, I was still contacting as many people as I could in the business with the idea of a possible job change. I don't know whether it was because I was so busy or whether I really had gotten Susan out of my system, but I was not even giving a thought to my love life, or lack of same. That is, until I saw Dr. Field again the following week. When she once more brought up the idea of going to a dating service, I again balked. My resistance was the same as most men's would be – It went something like: "What the hell do I need that for? I can find my own women. Besides, every time I've ever been 'fixed up' with someone, she turned out to be a disaster."

I tried to move on to other things, but Dr. Field wouldn't let me avoid the issue. She had several patients who had gone to a particular nationally recognized organization. They'd all been pleasantly surprised at the high quality of people they'd met. One lady even got married to a man she'd found through this service.

I kept coming up with reasons why I didn't want to get involved with the dating service, but Dr. Field seemed to have an answer to all of them. The biggest obstacle for me was the fear of wasting a lot of time and money meeting people with whom I had nothing in common. I told her what had happened when I'd gotten involved with a "computer match" outfit several years before. The three women I was "scientifically" paired with were an ex-WAC cook, a 250 pound criminal lawyer and a pimply faced teenager who lied on her application. Dr. Field had an answer for that too. This organization she was recommending had a system – A professional photographer took pictures of you which went into an album along with an extensive biography. And, they did a video taped interview of everyone. So, if you got a list of people who wanted to get in touch, you had an opportunity to come into the office and review all these materials before you said yes or no. And that went both ways. If you saw a video or a picture of someone you wanted to meet, that person had a chance to look you over before agreeing to get together.

I had to admit it sounded pretty good. Dr. Field succeeded in getting a commitment from me to investigate this dating outfit which, amazingly, I did that same day. I went right over to their offices, which were quite near Dr. Field's place, before I had a chance to chicken out. A very attractive young woman was very helpful and took me through the whole procedure. But I didn't sign up right away. I took an application home with me, which was quite extensive, to fill out. I started on it, but put it aside to get back to the pilot script. Then I dropped that to work on my own stuff. Then I put those things aside to watch TV. This quickly became a pattern for me – start to work on one thing, then put it aside for another, then distract myself with anything I could – phone calls to friends, long lunches, trips to the market, the book store – I even developed a sudden interest in pruning and fertilizing the plants in my yard. Before I knew it, I'd become a world class procrastinator. I was doing anything I could to keep myself from completing any work.

For a day or two I was actually pleased that I was finally relaxing enough to take the pressure off myself. But by the time I had my next appointment with Dr. Field the following week, it had become a real problem. I was getting anxious calls from work, asking me for my script. I couldn't make any appointments to present my semi-finished ideas. And, dust was gathering on my dating service application.

I'd fully intended to get right into this procrastination problem with Dr. Field, but I was even able to put that off by first telling her about going to the service she'd recommended. She was very pleased, but when I started prattling on, repeating myself, she got me back on track.

"Shawn, there's something you're holding back," she said.

I could no longer avoid the issue. I told her of my recent attack of "put-it-off-itis".

"I don't get it. When I left you last time, I really felt like we'd cleared away a lot of barriers. But now I seem to be playing all sorts of tricks on myself to keep from going ahead." Dr. Field smiled. "You probably won't believe this, but I think it's a healthy sign."

"What? You'll have to explain that one!"

"I believe you're right on the brink of a major breakthrough. The caterpillar in you senses that it soon will become a butterfly. And it's scary."

"Well, that's encouraging. But as much as I like putting a pretty face on it, I think there's something else at work here."

"Of course. You're dealing with big issues – looking for a new love and maybe a new job. That's always tough. Plus the fact that you've let go of a lot of emotional baggage that wasn't even your own."

"Oh, yeah," I agreed. "It's like I was a T.O.L. and suddenly lost a hundred pounds."

Dr. Field looked puzzled. "A 'T.O.L.'? What's that?"

"A Tub Of Lard."

"I never heard that expression before. But it's very apt. What you're saying is you don't recognize yourself yet. But you will."

SEVERING THE TIES 183

"But when? And when am I going to get off the dime and begin finishing what I start?"

"When do YOU think you will?"

"You did it to me again, didn't you?"

"What?"

"Turned my question around on me."

"Well, Shawn, only you know the answer to it."

She was right, of course. I scowled with frustration, but then something funny hit me and I laughed out loud.

"What are you laughing at?" Dr. Field inquired, looking baffled at my sudden change of mood.

"I don't know why, but I just thought of a remark of Fred Allen's. Do you remember Fred Allen?"

"Yes I do. He was a comedian."

"Allen had a running feud with Jack Benny and he was brilliant with put-downs. He once said of Jack, 'He has a thought preying on his sinuses, searching for his mind.' That's sort of the way I feel. I know the answer is somewhere in my head, but I feel like I'm stuck up my nose someplace looking for it."

Dr. Field assured me that I would find my way out of my nasal cavities in my own good time. But still, something wasn't right. It just seemed like there was some elusive factor that was holding me up and we were missing it. Dr. Field then asked me, "Do you think it might have anything to do with John?"

I couldn't think of any tie-in between John Williams and my procrastination problem, but as Sherlock Holmes used to say, when you've eliminated every possibility that is incorrect, the only one left must be the correct answer. So, even though I was apprehensive about revisiting John, particularly after my last experience, I asked Dr. Field to guide me back to do a bit of detective work. She performed her familiar induction procedure and I slipped back in time once again. Almost immediately I felt as though it might have been a mistake. I could hear gun fire and shell explosions off in the distance. I was back in the World War. I must have groaned or said something like, "Oh, no!" because Dr. Field asked me what was the matter.

"It's the bloody war. I can't get away from it."

"Is this John?"

"Yeah."

"Where are you?"

I opened my eyes and looked around. "I'm in hospital."

"The same hospital you were in before? The field hospital?"

"No. This is much better. Cleaner. Doesn't smell bad. I'm sitting here in the hallway in a wheel chair."

"Are you still in France?"

"Yeah. About thirty kilometers from the front. God, how I wish I could go home to England. But I have a problem with that – just a minute – the doctor's coming ..."

I could see a middle aged man in a white coat and a young nurse walking toward me from down the hall.

"What's the doctor doing?" asked Dr. Field.

"He's asking me how I feel."

"Oh, bloody awful, Doc! The pain never goes away. And I can't sleep. And my arm is useless. I can't even pick up a tea spoon..."

The doctor started feeling around my wound and I let out a holler. He wrote a few notes on my chart, then told the nurse to give me something for the pain. Then he moved on down the hall.

"So you're still feeling pretty bad?" asked Dr. Field.

"Yeah, but just between you, me and the lamppost, I'm laying it on a bit thick."

"Why is that?"

"Well, the war is almost over. But I'm afraid they might send me back to the front if they think I'm recovering too fast. I reckon if I can stall them long enough they'll send me home."

"You really think they'd send you back to fight with a wound like yours?"

"I've seen them do that and worse."

"And you don't think this is shirking your duty?"

This really made me angry. "Shirk my duty?" I bellowed. "Well, let me tell you, I've been in this war from the very beginning, up to my neck in mud and blood and shit. I've seen more agony, more death, more destruction – I've done my part and then some! I've had my fill! There's no reason why I or anybody else should shed another drop of our life's blood in this God damned insanity!"

"Alright. Alright. I understand. So this stalling is actually a matter of life and death. It means your very survival."

"You got that right."

"That's very enlightening. Well, John, I'm sure you'll be going home soon. I think we'll say goodbye now."

"Goodbye to you."

Dr. Field brought me slowly back to consciousness. We were both excited at uncovering what seemed to be an obvious link between my putting things off and John's dragging out his illness. We discussed this enthusiastically for the remaining moments of the hour.

It seemed quite clear now that my unconscious attempt to postpone my professional and personal affairs was also a kind of survival device. I was trying to perpetuate an old life that was coming to an end – hardly as frightening or dramatic as a war-weary, wounded soldier attempting to stay alive, but still a very big deal. By uncovering John's holding action, Dr. Field and I felt confident I had severed its influence on my life's activities. To repeat what I'd said previously to her, I had enough to handle without carrying John's baggage too.

As I drove home, my spirits soared. I was exhilarated as I threw open my front door – I couldn't wait to get to work. Didn't even want to eat dinner. But on the way into my office I noticed I had a message on my answering machine. It took the wind out of my sails fast. It was a call from the studio legal department. Would I come in tomorrow at 11:00 AM to discuss "restructuring my deal"? In Hollywood legal-speak that usually meant one thing – take a hike.

From the Therapist's Perspective

"The journey through life, or lifetimes,
is truly a journey within,
a meandering deep into one's being.
Sometimes paths separate, sometimes they blend.
The link of lives comes together and then moves apart
but through it all we progress and grow."
—Kahlil Gibran, *The Prophet*

Shawn was like the caterpillar. He had woven his own cocoon, and in that chrysalis state, was preparing for his rebirth. Yet, he was not aware of what was happening nor was he ready for self delivery. Nevertheless he was having huge labor pains. Eventually, like the butterfly, he would break through his newly formed womb and experience a kind of rebirth.

Comparing them to a good Irish stew, many of the significant ingredients of his and John's lives were well blended together — the stab in the chest from the German soldier, the wound to his heart brought about by Susan, the terror and trauma of the battlefield, the chaos and confusion created by the earthquake, and now the trauma of the threat of Shawn's being cut off from his job. Shawn and I needed to separate the stuff in the pot so that each ingredient could be tasted alone. Then we'd have a truce from the war within his head which was "shaking me (him) crazy inside." I pondered for awhile over Shawn's physical stab by that German soldier and Shawn's mental wound brought about by Susan. The physical pain appeared to be the same; the pain in his chest was very intense.

Each time I went into a trance state with Shawn, as the guiding hypnotherapist tends to do, I seemed to become more on the same wavelength with him. I truly believe if we could have viewed our brain waves on a monitor, they would be doing a similar dance and somehow be joined.

I had a sense that if I once again utilized the passage of my hands over Shawn's chest, as I did in that initial session when John first emerged, maybe my original intention to relieve

Shawn of his pain would once more be realized. How could I re-enact this most effectively, now?

Molly came to my mind. She had helped John bury Maggie. Maybe now Molly could assist in symbolically putting Susan to rest. I smiled to myself as the word "yiskadol" came into my head, the Hebrew word which begins the mourner's prayer.

I used verbal hypnotic techniques along with the passing of my hands to bring Shawn once more back to John's persona. As I had John create a most tranquil and peaceful scenario in the comfort of his own abode, I brought good ole' Molly back into the picture. She (I) moved her fingers over his chest in a most soothing, comforting, and relaxing manner. The suggestion was that the pain "would melt away, melt like butter or ice cream on a hot summer's day".

When I brought Shawn back into a state of awareness, I held my breath as I asked him, "How do you feel, Shawn?" His response brought about an answer I had hoped to hear. He felt "much better". And yes, he was "wrung out" or exhausted from the experience. Of course he was. He had let go of a lot of stuff. I somehow had the sensation that the resulting effort was not only the release of the pain not even his physician could alleviate, but also the relinquishing of Susan. Shawn finally got her off his chest.

"Now what in that stew needs to be ladled up next?" I thought to myself after giving Shawn some positive reinforcements for the extraordinary work he had done to this point.

John had explained a good deal. Now was the time to cut him loose. John's carry-on baggage contained a lot of garments for Shawn to wear, and now that Shawn was no longer naked, he could find his own clothes. We could send the rest of his luggage back into the past by way of Concorde jet.

The emotional load of both John and Shawn was too much for one man to carry. So, without the use of hypnosis, I decided to separate the two men. I repeated, "Shawn, today is not John; maybe yesterday, but not today." Thus, we began to look at the lives of John and Shawn and how what happened in each of their lives was different. Together, we noted some key differences between the two personas. We reviewed the list. Shawn began with John's drinking as opposed to his (Shawn's) being a teetotaler. We snaked around through John's having been severely wounded in the war versus Shawn's never having been in active service, moved toward the abandonment issue differences, and finally were caught up in the net of John's Maggie and Shawn's Susan. For Shawn, this rang a bell, a very loud "oops" bell. True, both men had difficulty in letting go of their lost loves. Nevertheless, I believed Shawn was ready to move on. He was "at the bottom of that page". I then shared with Shawn what my sixth sense had relayed to me — that when Molly relieved his pain, she had also taken away his "heartache", resulting in her literally having moved Susan "off his chest".

As the grandfather clock chimed the hour, Shawn departed that session. It was as though the clock was cheering at what had occurred in this most valuable meeting. In fact, its six piercing notes that marked 6:00 PM seemed to sever the chord between Shawn's life and that of John's very sad and dreadful existence.

Shawn left expressing his need to "mull over" and "digest". Indeed, therapy does not end in the psychologist's office. Rather, it goes on in ones head between sessions. As with Shawn on some occasions, the session set the groundwork for some further self-hypnosis or self-therapy to take place at home. More often, when pieces of the puzzle begin to fit in the therapy session, and since the brain never stops processing, the puzzle is often completed between the sessions without any effort on the patient's part. On other occasions, the patient unknowingly makes it happen by pondering over "stuff" in somewhat of a trance state while sitting in one's favorite chair or when lying in bed. He often comes up with more material or makes decisions based on the therapy. Behavior modification occurs at some point, resulting in new and different kinds of functioning.

When Shawn arrived for his session on the following week, he began by announcing that he had obtained a form from the dating service I had recommended. I was pleased to hear that he had taken action toward meeting other women. Yes, indeed Shawn was moving on, having cut loose from Susan. He was manifesting what I just referred to as *behavior modification*.

However, Shawn, soon began to double talk and roam down several irrelevancies. "Beating around the bush", it's often called.

For me that meant he was avoiding. What was he not wanting to tell me?

When I got him out from the bush and back on the road, he told me of his "put-it-off-itis". He believed he was "playing tricks" — to keep from going ahead. It was hard for Shawn to believe that I saw this as a healthy sign. Change is scary.

My mind went back to Malaysia and the butterfly farm I visited there. Among the beautiful, colorful, huge butterflies, on the branch of a tree, a little cocoon was pulsing like a tiny heart. My private guide had pointed out how the caterpillar inside this formation was about to be reborn as a butterfly. The pulsations were that of its labor; soon it would deliver itself. I wondered at that time if that little creature was having labor pains as it completed its transformation.

Since I often think in terms of the butterfly, I saw Shawn's struggling like that insect, perhaps experiencing the pain of his labor which would complete his transformation.

But Shawn felt there was even something more, and the patient knows best. Was there another link to sever from John, I thought? I asked Shawn if it would be OK to explore that aspect. With Shawn's permission, we once again returned to the past. In coming upon John, there he was, in the hospital recovering from his wound and pretending to be in a worse condition than he actually was. John explained that his purpose was to avoid being sent back to active duty. He's wanting to "stall them long enough so they'll send me home". To John, the stalling was, as I declared and to which he agreed, "a matter of life and death — his very survival".

After saying goodbye to John, I brought Shawn out of trance. Yes, we were very excited that there was more than an apparent link to Shawn's stalling. Just the fact that he went back to that particular "John scene" on that very date was significant. We were looking for an answer to why he was putting things off and we came upon John's malingering with the pain and suffering from his wound.

Understanding this was all that Shawn needed to let go of his procrastination. Shawn's was also a matter of survival, *survival* of his own old life. No matter how miserable one's way of life may be, it is difficult to give up that to which one is accustomed. We are creatures of habit. That is what makes change so difficult. Taking a new form and traveling a different road is also frightening. We feel vulnerable and alone as we take that turn onto the unknown highway which begins the journey. We mourn what we have just left behind.

As Shawn gave up his old life, he was, at the same time, saying a final farewell to John. So much of Shawn's old behavior seemed to be the result of what had occurred so many years earlier with John. Maybe the unfinished business with John was meant to be completed by Shawn. Some talk about "lessons yet to be learned". And maybe giving up two lives at once made it even harder on Shawn.

By the way, I never knew and I still wonder if John had ever married Molly. Shawn never went back to any scene which indicated anything about that, one way or the other. I guess we'll never know. I do believe that Shawn had, that day, sliced away the last of the old and was on the way to the new. He left my office in the highest of spirits — his face more brightly lit than I had ever seen before. He appeared to beam with excitement and the motivation to move forward.

I had such good feelings as Shawn departed. As for Shawn, too bad, on that very day, upon arriving home, he was to be confronted by the message that lay in waiting on his answering machine. That was no way to begin a new life.

XII

The Hero's Journey

Crowning Celebration

Conflict

Resolution

Pit of Despair

XII

THE HERO'S JOURNEY

*M*y meeting with the studio legal department was one of those good-news, bad-news mixed messages. The good news was that they wanted to continue the deal I had. The bad news was they wanted to extend it only until the end of the year. After that they would "reevaluate" the situation. At least I knew where I stood for the next six months, which by today's standards in the animation business is a lifetime. So I got back to work on studio business and my preparations for a likely job change. Meanwhile, I finally got around to filling out the application and writing my bio for the dating service. They signed me up and took my money. That was followed by a photo session and a video taped interview which left me with nervous sweat rings under my arms the size of two truck tires. But considering what they had to work with, the pictures and the tape both came out reasonably well. My smiling face and my terribly witty biography were placed in the "R" (for Regan) catalogue and my tape went onto the archive shelf with a code number attached to it. I was now officially "available".

Before I'd even had a chance to look at potential dates, I received a notice by mail that five women, obviously ladies of great taste, wanted to meet me. I went over to the dating service office and scoped them out. They all seemed quite attractive.

I picked out one of the five and called her. I met Sheri for coffee. Very nice, but no sparks.

Now, instead of being chosen by someone else, I decided to pick out some women I wanted to contact. I gave their names to the girl at the desk, went home and waited. And waited. None of them replied! My ego felt like a bruise on a piece of overripe fruit. But in the meantime, I received another notice that four more women wanted to make my acquaintance. This time I made coffee dates with two of them – Stephanie and Erica. Again, both very sweet, but we had little in common and no physical attraction. So, once more it was my turn to choose. This time I got one response, but of all the women I'd met thus far, Lisa was by far the most incompatible. Very good looking, but all she could talk about was her rotten ex-husband.

I began to get discouraged, which I reported to Dr. Field the next time I saw her. She was a bit testy with me.

"Oh, come on, Shawn! You've only been in the program for three or four weeks. Give it some time."

Which I did. Over the next two months I met at least ten more women. Most of them I only saw once. Two of them I dated for short periods of time. I had a brief but very intense interlude with one – Arlene. But as the lyrics to the Cole Porter song say, "It was too hot not to cool down." Why it suddenly went cold I don't know, but for once in my life I was not going to drag things out just because I didn't want to be the one who ended it. I was proud of myself for being able to tell her I felt it was over. "Plenty of other fish in the sea," I thought to myself, and even more at the dating service. I went there the very next day to pick someone new. Unfortunately, so did Arlene. Running into her there was a 10+ on the embarrassment scale. Even now, years later, I get a twinge thinking about it. I believe John Williams would have run right out and got drunk.

Meanwhile, Dr. Field and I continued to meet once a week. We revisited John Williams three or four more times over the next couple of months, but none of the regressions lasted more than a few minutes. In one I found myself as an eight or nine year old John being frightened by viewing a fox hunt. Apparently there was a hunt club near the orphanage, and John, who had wandered out into the woods close by, had something of a narrow escape as he was nearly run down by galloping horses ridden by men in red hats and jackets.

In another regression, I discovered my John Williams self in a hotel room with a prostitute. This kind of situation had come up before and is described in an earlier chapter. But on this occasion, John was much younger, only about fifteen years old. It was probably his first sexual experience with a woman and it was a disaster. John was so nervous he couldn't get it up. He left feeling very frustrated and humiliated.

By the end of summer, Dr. Field and I had concluded our trips to another life with John Williams. It had become more and more difficult to connect with John, and from a therapeutic standpoint, there didn't seem to be much point in continuing to go back anymore. The lines that tied the sad and traumatic events of John Williams' life to mine had pretty much been severed. Whatever problems I continued to have, and there were a few, were now mine and mine alone.

Meantime, almost four months had gone by since I'd joined the dating service, and I was beginning to think of it as Dorothy Parker did of Hollywood – that there was "no there there". And it didn't make matters any easier when I would occasionally get a call from Susan. She was just being friendly, staying in touch, but every time she'd say goodbye, I would have "hello again" on my mind for several days afterward. I felt like I was slipping backward.

Then, one day I received a letter via the dating service. It contained a note from someone who would change my life. Her name was Deborah King. Her message was so intelligently and sweetly written that I immediately responded. We chatted on the phone, then agreed to meet at a local restaurant the following Friday night.

Someone once said that all great things begin badly. It certainly was the case with Deborah and me. I drove around for what seemed hours trying to find the place where we were supposed to meet. By the time I got to the restaurant, almost an hour late, I was grumpier than Scrooge. It turned out that Deborah, who had never been to this eatery either, had been given the wrong address by a friend. She arrived just minutes ahead of me. It was amazing that either of us found it. Or each other. And it was even more amazing that Deborah wouldn't think that I was a foulmouthed lowbrow instead of a mild mannered cartoon writer. I blew my cork. The place was nearly empty, and yet, because we didn't have a reservation, we were told there were no tables available. I let loose with a few choice expletives for our charmless host, grabbed Deborah's hand and left. Fortunately, there was another restaurant in the same mall complex, so in we went and sat down to get acquainted. As I cooled off, I really warmed up to Deborah. If being gorgeous were music, she was a symphony orchestra – blonde, blue-eyed and beautiful. But her personality and sense of humor were what really grabbed me. I usually attribute a "great sense of humor" to anyone who laughs at my jokes, but in Deborah's case it went way beyond that. She had me rolling in my chicken salad with her stories of her family in Minnesota, her tennis playing friends and her work associates. Deborah was also a writer, but her work was as far from cartoons as Seattle is from Miami. She was employed by a large medical insurance firm, doing promotional and technical writing. "Collateral" was the industry jargon for her product. But as dry as that sounds, I later learned when reading her stuff, what a genius she was at making the dull delightful.

Needless to say, I was hooked from the very get-go. I never again dated another woman. As a matter of fact, I rushed right over to the dating service and put myself out of the running. Deborah was the one for me. That was over five years ago and we've been together ever since. On May 14, 2000, we were married.

Every time I think of how much I had to change in order to reach the point where I could relate to someone the way I do to Deborah, I have to believe in miracles. When I focus in on the fact that I'm not a young man, I'd never been married, never even lived with a woman, I have to wonder what it was that allowed me to make such a drastic turnaround. It was much more likely that I would win the state lottery than it was that I would ever have a really close, intimate, committed relationship with a woman. I can only conclude, as I said earlier, that I was indeed carrying around someone else's baggage. Being able to jettison John Williams's steamer trunk full of sorrows must have been the determining factor.

So my personal life has changed radically for the better. But what about my "soul storms"? How am I dealing with what was once a morbid, overwhelming fear of nature's forces? First of all, I readily admit that earthquakes still scare me... me and the rest of the world. And I'm not ashamed to admit I'm also afraid of the "devil winds". They can be very destructive, and after all, I didn't make up the name. But what about my crippling dread of rain? Not hurricanes or floods or monsoons, but the terror that even the slightest sprinkle could cause – the gut wrenching panic that came out of nowhere – the thing that drove me to seek out Dr. Field in the first place – did all the therapy and all the past life regressions have any lasting effect on that?

The answer to that question I think can best be given by relating what happened during the "El Nino" rains in the early months of 1998. Every night and day for almost a year, it seemed, we were being warned on the news of the havoc this phenomenon was going to wreak on North America – particularly California. It was a TV weather forecaster's bonanza, almost as overblown as the Clinton/Lewinski affair. "Look out!" "It's coming!" "Got flood insurance?" "Get your sandbags ready!" "Head for the high ground!" "Better get started on that ark!" The media was promoting "El Nino" like a disaster film. I got to the point where I would go out of my way to avoid all these apostles of meteorologic Armageddon. I stopped reading the paper. I wouldn't listen to my car radio. I even began to prefer infomercials to newscasts. All this constant trumpeting of impending cataclysms was driving even normal people up the wall.

November came and went without much rain. So did December. And then January. Still hardly any inclement weather at all. I was beginning to think that maybe El Nino was as sick of its hype as I was. Maybe we'd get through the winter unscathed. But, like any good horror movie, just when you thought you were safe, the monster descended upon us with a vengeance.

I firmly believe the reason there are only twenty-eight days in February is because it is the rottenest month of the year and the people who designed our calendar wanted it to be over as fast as possible – a decision with which I heartily concur. February of 1998 was an even more colossal stinker than usual. The long vaunted El Nino rains finally arrived, causing floods all over the western United States and particularly in Southern California. Day after day I was outside, dressed only in a badly fitting bathing suit and carrying an old pink umbrella, cursing a blue streak as I siphoned the water that was filling up my back yard through hoses stretched to the gutter in front of my house. I made a cute picture, squatting at the curb, showing my plumbers' crack to the world while sucking my guts out to get the water flowing into the street, and at the same time trying to keep at least some of the downpour off my shivering body. This scenario was repeated at least a dozen times during the course of the month. I was in a constantly foul mood, spitting out obscenities when I wasn't spitting out brackish rainwater. I hated this process worse than having a colonoscopy with barbed wire.

It was only when the worst of the storms subsided several weeks later that a 5000 watt light bulb went on inside my head. All through this period, weather that would have previously frozen me in my tracks with fear had instead mobilized me. I'd been so pissed off at the inconvenience and the mess that I'd forgotten to be scared! Well, okay, not completely. I mean, I wasn't like some dimwit who gets on a surfboard as a hurricane is approaching. But whatever trepidation I had was far outbalanced by my wrath.

I guess we can argue about what the right response to an El Nino situation should be. After all, the storms caused millions of dollars in damage, destroying homes, roads, crops, and even killed a number of people. But for me personally, if I have a choice between being petrified with fright or blowing my stack, I'll take the latter every time. I believe that El Nino was a test I passed with flying colors.

The next question is, of course, was this all an elaborate mind game I played on myself, or was it what it appeared to be – a return to another existence? *Was John Williams a real person?*

I sidestepped this question for quite a long time. For one thing, it all seemed so bizarre. Even spooky. I mean, what if I did find that John Williams had actually lived? Could I deal with that? For another thing, I have no research skills. When I was a kid, there was a radio character called, "Mr. Keen, Tracer Of Lost Persons". When he died, my only contact with anyone adept at tracking down people died with him. I had no idea how to even trace a tracer, let alone a person who may have died two thirds of a century ago.

However, despite my uneasiness and my archival ignorance, curiosity kept nibbling away at me – did John really exist and if so, could I prove it? Then one day, I don't remember who mentioned it to me, but I was told that the Mormon Church keeps the most extensive records of any organization in the world. Most of their files are housed in Utah, but they also have a very large microfilm library on the grounds of the Mormon Cathedral in West Los Angeles. I called them up and was invited to come over and see what I could find.

I had a fairly good idea of when John was born – somewhere between 1892 and 1897 – but not where. Although it was probably in the London area, it could have been anywhere in England. This avenue quickly proved hopeless, because birth records were scant. They just weren't very thorough back in the 1890's at keeping track of who had whom and when.

The next thing I checked were the death records. I was fairly certain that John died in London sometime in the early 1930's and would have been anywhere between thirty-four and forty years of age. But there were literally hundreds of John Williams listed who passed away at this time. And, while the ages of some were listed, most were not. I looked at roll after roll of microfilm – row after row of men named John Williams – the more records I looked at, the more baffled I became. There were just too many of him. I began to feel quite discouraged. But then a very nice lady librarian named Annie came over. Sensing my consternation, she asked if she could help me find something. I gave her a rough sketch of John Williams and what I thought I knew about his vital stats. She suggested that if I really wanted a detailed search, there were a number of other sources that could be accessed. Unfortunately, most of these were in England. But there were expert people on this side of the Atlantic who, for a fee, could do the job for me. She gave me the name and phone number of a woman in Utah named Florence Jessop whom she knew personally. I called her that evening.

Florence was very eager to take up the challenge. For the next two months, while she dug, Florence and I kept in touch by phone and E-Mail. But the job was even bigger than she had first believed. She and her associate in London checked marriage records, hospital records, pension records and probate records, among others. They came up with many John Williams who were almost right, but not quite. One of them seemed very close to the mark, however – John H. Williams, age 38, who died in Chelsea. There is a large military hospital, barracks and old soldiers' home there, and John, a wounded veteran and probably in ill health for a period before his passing, might well have been going there for treatment. This could account for his being on a train platform. I got very excited about this discovery until I looked closer at the date of his death – December, 1936 – eight months after my own birth. I'm assuming that the transmigration of a soul takes place before one is born, not after. But, maybe not. Maybe John was nursing a hangover and arrived late. Anyway, I put this one aside when Florence came up with another possibility.

The death certificate from St. Barts' Hospital in London reads that a John Williams, age 44, died in London May 24, 1935. Ages were usually estimated and John, a heavy drinker, probably looked older than he was. The cause is listed as "General Apoplexy" – which could be anything sudden, like a stroke. He is also listed as having kidney disease, which would be consistent with an alcoholic. It's conceivable that he had a seizure while standing on the station platform and fell to the rails, but no mention is made of it.

Florence turned up several others, all of whom died around the early and mid-1930's, but for one reason or another, none of them seemed to be a close enough match. But she did come up with a very interesting marriage record. The certificate reads: John Williams, bachelor, age 20, married Martha Ellen Rodley, age 20, at St. Patrick's Roman Catholic Church in Leeds, England, August 28, 1915. Martha's father is listed as a boot finisher, something our John had in common with him. But there are a few inconsistencies. First, John's occupation is listed as a "munitions worker", not a soldier. Perhaps that was John's specialty in the army, but it's a stretch. Secondly, the bride's name is not "Maggie", although Martha could possibly have been nicknamed "Mattie" which I construed as "Maggie" – but that's also questionable.

I suppose I could have kept Florence working for months on a search for a perfect match. Unfortunately, cartoon writers don't make the kind of money it requires to finance the many hours it takes to sift through hundreds if not thousands of documents. So, for the time being, there it stands. But who knows? Maybe one of those mentioned here is indeed the genuine article. If not, maybe someday we'll have another go at finding him.

But whether or not I can ever prove that I lived as John Williams in another incarnation, I know that the regressions through which Dr. Field guided me were as real as any experiences I've ever had. Real because they changed my ability to connect on a profoundly emotional level, and real because they were the critical factor in relieving me of my *"Brain Storms"*. Before going through these adventures in another man's life and in another man's body, I couldn't relate to a woman in any depth and I had a terrible phobia. I now have a wonderful lady and I don't go to pieces when the sky clouds up. I'm a happier man and hopefully a better man. **That's the reality that matters to me.**

From the Therapist's Perspective

"...Long have we sailed on the perilous seas,
and we have climbed the steepest mountains
and we have wrestled with the storms.
We have known hunger,
but we have also sat at wedding feasts.
Oftentimes have we been naked,
but we have also worn kingly raiment.
We have indeed traveled far..."
—Kahlil Gibran, *The Garden of the Prophet*

Shawn has completed an incredible journey! It was a voyage extraordinaire! As in any spectacular hero's adventure, whether it be myth, a folk tale, fantasy or fable, Shawn traveled the ellipse which is called *The Hero's Journey*. This *Passage* begins with a major *Conflict* which goes downhill until the poor, wretched soul finds himself in the *Pit of Despair*. The hero finally gasps for breath, and reaching both arms outward, pulls himself out of the pit and begins his quest for the *Holy Grail*, the *Key* which will emancipate his soul. He then moves in a new direction to a profound *Resolution* or *Rebirth*. The finale is sometimes culminated with a *Crowning Celebration*.

With his dreadful fear of windy, rainy weather, Shawn begins *The Hero's Journey*. His environmental anguish escalates with his response to the Northridge quake, while Susan's reception to his quakey and quacky behavior throws him even deeper into the *Pit of Despair*.

Two weeks prior to the Northridge disaster, Shawn's chest pains lead him into the Discovery Channel where he encounters John Williams, his Self from the past. As we first view John, he is in the battlefront trenches of *"The* World War". His chest has just been brutally pierced by a German soldier's bayonet. He is, without a doubt, in deep and excruciating pain.

Shawn's life, is an echo of John's old world. John becomes the *Key* to the door of transformation by which Shawn's life is turned around. In John's being, Shawn not only finds the causative factors for his dread of wind and rain, but also discovers the source of his fear of intimacy. Furthermore, John holds the *Key* to some of Shawn's physical problems.

Having discovered, comprehended, and "worked through" the events and the feelings involved with his past Self, Shawn has arrived at the *Turning Point* of his passage. At this juncture, he must learn how to disengage from John's ego. With this separation, Shawn has attained the *Resolution* phase of his journey. He is now, as I say in therapy, "Free Forever", from the fears that once plagued him. Like the hero of any mythical tale, Shawn has been *Reborn*. He now lives without concern about when or what the God of Thunder will hurl down upon him. He also dwells with a beautiful lady, Deborah, who has become his bride. Their wedding was the *Crowning Celebration*.

Fantasy, fact, or fiction — who can tell? A Hero's Journey, for sure. As Shawn declares — *"That's the reality that matters to me."*

Epilogue

Fantasy, fact or fiction — who can tell?
It's "The reality" that rings the bell.
Shawn has come full circle, without a doubt,
Keying into what John Williams was all about.
John's escapades were back in Hell,
And from his drinking, he finally fell.
We thank him, however, for all he had given,
That made Shawn an echo of what John was livin'.
Goodbye now to John and rainy, windy weather.
Like with a bayonet, all these Brain Storms we sever.
As for Shawn, a new life he lives.
And to Deborah, his true love he gives.

As an Author

Dr. Eleanor S. Field is also co-author
of the Literary Guild selection:
The Good Girl Syndrome
(Macmillan, 1985)
(Berkley Books, 1987)
This book was later translated and
published in Japan, Germany, Brazil,
Argentina, and the U.K.

Dr. Field has also authored numerous
scientific publications.

As an Author

Dr. Field's patient, the hero of this book, is the real life counterpart of Shawn Regan. He has been a professional writer for more than thirty years.

The majority of his creative efforts has been in animation. He has worked with many studios including Warner Brothers, Hanna-Barbera, and Nickelodeon. His work has received a Peabody award, an Academy Award nomination, and three Emmy nominations.

About the Pen Name
—Shawn Regan

To maintain anonymity, the hero chose the name Shawn Regan.

Shawn Regan was a character in the classic movie, *The Big Sleep*. Starring Lauren Bacall and Humphrey Bogart, the character Shawn Regan was a dominant figure throughout the movie. However, he never appeared on the screen!

About the Symbol

This clockwise spiral (starting from the middle) is strongly associated with *water, power, independent movement*, and *outgoing migrations of tribes*. The ideogram is primarily a sign illustrating *movement*.

The Vikings used it with the meaning, *independent movement*, against the sun, waves and wind, and eventual *return* or *homecoming*. It appeared as a form for the sternposts on their ships.

A similar sign has been used for over 4000 years as decoration on the clothes of kings, high priests, and gods and goddesses represented as statues in many different cultures.

Just as ancient cultures utilized images, so too is our present society become more imagery conscious. Thinking in images takes one to a metaphorical level, which, like dreaming, can bring pleasure to one's soul.

About the Illustrations

Julie Welch created both the cover art and the icons preceding each chapter. Her natural creativity and skills as an artist were enhanced by a formal education in art. She is presently combining "making a fortune" with "making a difference" as the owner of the Yoni Tattoo salon in Tarzana, California.

Cover:

The *trance-formation* of Shawn and his *Brain Storms!* From dark clouds ...to a world of brilliant sunshine.

I   Looking for the key to unlock Shawn's many problems.

II   John Williams in the trenches *In "The" War.*

III   John's returning home and receiving traumatic news.

IV   John's falling to the tracks below.

V   The train's carrying Shawn back in time.

VI   Nature's revenge.

VII Shawn's "letting go".

VIII John's approach to the music publisher.

IX   Shawn's packing his trunk full of problems to throw overboard.

X   John's "burying" Maggie.

XI   Shawn's *Severing the Ties.*

XII *The Hero's Journey.*

About the Type

Typesetting for **Brain Storms!** utilized the typefaces *Boulevard* and *ITC Zapf Chancery* for the title and initial caps. Designed in 1979 by Hermann Zapf, *ITC Zapf Chancery* is a contemporary script based on Italian Chancery handwriting. The Chancery hand was developed during the Italian Renaissance and originally used for formal and informal work by the scribes in the papal offices.

The *ITC Caslon 224* type family was used for the main body of the text and headers. *ITC Caslon 224* was produced by Ed Benguiat for the International Typeface Corporation in 1983.

Helvetica was used for headlines and to delineate the start of Dr. Elly's sections. *Helvetica* was created in 1957 by Max Miedinger for the Haas foundry of Switzerland. The name comes from *Helvetia*, the Latin name for Switzerland. The design is based on the grotesques of the late nineteenth century. Lastly, *ITC Zapf Dingbats* was chosen for bullets.